THE NEWEST

FROM CALIFORNIA

THE NEWEST LOGO

FROM CALIFORNIA

2

WITHDRAWN

PUBLISHED BY NIPPAN

First Published in Germany by:
NIPPAN
Nippon Shuppan Hanbai
Deutschland GmbH
Krefelder Str. 85
D-40549 Düsseldorf
Telephone: (0211) 5048089
Fax: (0211) 5049326

ISBN 3-910052-17-1

Design by: Harish Patel Design, New York

Printed in Hong Kong

ACKNOWLEDGMENTS

This series was started by Gerry Rosentswieg in 1992. Our collaboration lasted until his death in 1995. It was his inspiration and his inventiveness that allowed me the courage to attempt this project without him. For this and countless other kindnesses and dreams we shared, I thank him, publicly.

Contents

designer   Jeanine Colini
illustrator   Patsy Tucker
design firm   Jeanine Colini Design
     Associates
client   Training With
     Tambourine
     Logo for animal
     behavioral specialists.

designer Paul Weingartner
art directors Steve Turner
Joan Hausman
design firm Hausman Design
client Altera
Mark for a semi-conductor programming company.

designer Paul Morales
design firm Onyx Design Inc.
client Birkenstock
Logo for back-to-school shoes and sandals.

designer Lissa Patrizi
design firm Patrizi Designs
client Jeff's Decorative Finishes
Logo for custom painting and art furniture.

(opposite)

designers Larry Vigon
Rowena Curtis
design firm Vigon/Ellis
client Can't Sing Can't Dance Productions
Logo for a television production company.

Introduction

Before the world was filled with people who could read, pictures were used to replace words. Those who sold goods or services hung pictures depicting what they did over their doors. These, then, were the first brandmarks and the first logos. While these informational symbols (pictures) were a necessity for thousands of years, today we have more sophisticated ways of passing on the same information. The old signs are now much sought after as antiques or simply as pleasing wall decor.

As more of the goods and services we needed were offered by many more tradesmen it became important to be able to distinguish one maker from the next. Letters and words would do the trick but few were literate and, as in America, many were literate but in some other language. It was but a short step to using symbols to identify which tradesman had made which product or offered which service. They became easy to identify and sometimes carried a message for those who could read.

The earliest marks were very straightforward, but as more competition developed the

mark expanded to include humor, puns, satire and even whimsy slipped into some. Fred Cooper's symbol for the New York Edison Company was dropped in the name of progress, but Mr. Peanut is still with us and still looking through his monocle. Both were used to identify a product and both used a light touch.

Isaac Newton said "For every action there is reaction." It is also true that each period of art is a reaction to the period that preceded it. Graphic design is no exception. The styles favored in the late 1800s and the early 1900s were more like personal statements. The fine work done in France and England during the Edwardian era, along with the Viennese Secessionist movement, were all hands-on movements. With the Armistice came Art Deco, a style that captured the imagination with a cross between the mechanical shapes of the draftsman and the artist's irrepressible spirits.

As the great depression was ending, some remarkable marks began to appear. They were strong, clever, highly imaginative and subjective. They have stood the test of time very well and one would be hard pressed today to tell a mark created in 1936 from one right out of today's computer. Since that time the trademark has grown increasingly refined and distilled.

As the larger companies expanded into new and more diversified markets the graphics they chose became less related to the companies' beginnings and were in some cases abstract. The most used logos of the

TM

designer   Mamoru Shimokochi
art director Anne Reeves
design firm   Shimokochi/Reeves
client   S/R Marketing Man
                Logo for identity and
                package design
                consultants.

time were difficult to identify— they were abstractions that reveal nothing about the identity of the company they represented.

Within the last decade things began to change. Humor and whimsy and the craft of graphic design began to slip back into the picture. The "NEW" logo is now, the marks are more quirky; what's new is beginning to look a lot like what's old. The charm and personality of the past has a decidedly "NOW" look and flavor. "NOW" is more eclectic, more colorful and more subjective.

As the nineties were starting to age, Rosentswieg was quoted as saying "The new logo is not necessarily a new phenomenon. There have always been those marks, usually created for small, creative companies that relied upon personality, wit and charm. Often the marks were created for designers and agencies for self promotion. But today, led by the music and entertainment industries, and followed closely by the clothing and computer industries, the NEW logo is appearing more often." These observations and ideas are now more mainstream; logos are again making a statement about whom or what they represent, and some of the world's largest companies now *believe.*

The Publisher

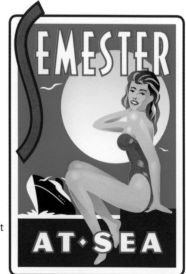

designer	Rod Dyer
design firm	Dyer/Mutchnick Group Inc.
client	Rooster Entertainment Group
	Logo for promoting the fun and romance of studying abroad.

1
designer   Glenn Sakamoto
art director Rod Dyer
design firm   Dyer/Mutchnick Group Inc.
client   J.H. Rothschild, Inc.
                Logo for a set and prop designer.

2
designer   Glenn Martinez
design firm   Glenn Martinez and Associates
client   J.M. Hershey Inc.
                Logo for a general contractor
                specializing in church building and
                remodeling.

3
designer   Julia Chong Tam
design firm   Julia Tam Design
client   Italian Hotel Reservation Center
                Logo for tourist services.

4
designer   Konrad Bright
design firm   Bright Strategic Design
client   Folb Construction
                Logo for building contractors
                and management.

5
designer   Ron Miriello
illustrator   Michelle Aranda
design firm   Miriello Grafico, Inc.
client   National University
                Logo for the university.

6
designer   Cheryl Pelly
design firm   Pelly Design Associates
client   St. Maximillian Kolbe
                Logo for a church.

1

2

J.M. HERSHEY INC.

ITALIAN HOTEL
RESERVATION CENTER

3

4

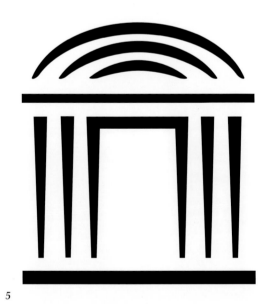

5

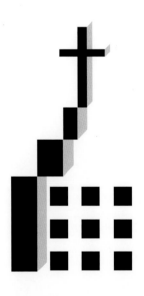

6

7
designer Cheryl Pelly
design firm Pelly Design Associates
client Citicopters News Service
Logo for news filming in
Los Angeles.

8
designer Eric Watanabe
art director Patti Judd
design firm Juddesign
client The Paragon Foundation
Logo for the parent company of
California Lutheran Homes and
Lutheran Social Services.

9
designer Archie Ong
design firm Inhaus Design
client Relocation Services
Logo for home relocation
services for employees of
large corporations.

10
designer Glenn Martinez
design firm Glenn Martinez and Associates
client Avalon Natural Cosmetics
Logo for a health and beauty
products company.

11
designer Konrad Bright
design firm Bright Strategic Design
client Terranova Construction
Logo for a construction company.

12
designers Philippe Becker
Primo Angeli
design firm Primo Angeli Inc.
client Rubin Glickman, Attorney
Logo highlights the landmark art
deco building that houses Rubin
Glickman's office.

13
designer Adrianna Dinihanian
design firm Pine Point Design
client Wrapworks
Logo for a take-out and
eat-in "wrap" (international
burrito) restaurant.

7

8   9

10

11

12

13

14
designer Julia Chong Tam
design firm Julia Tam Design
client AccuSight
Logo for a laser eye care center.

15
designer Richard Patterson
art director Mark Bergman
design firm SBG Partners
client Brown & Towland
Logo for a health care provider.

16
designers Jeanne Namkung
Anthony Luk
art directors Kenichi Nishiwaki
Russell Baker
design firm Profile Design
client FutureTel, Inc.
Logo for a multi-media technology provider.

17
designer Jeff Kahn
design firm Kahn Design
client BioMax
Logo for a colloidal nutritional
supplement.

18
designer Rod Dyer
design firm Dyer/Mutchnick Group Inc.
client Sony Pictures High Definition Center
Logo signifies one film process
moving to the other.

14

15

16

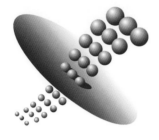 BioMax™

17

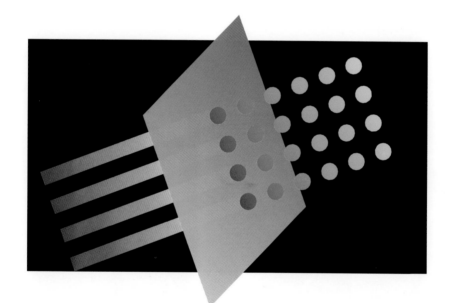

SONY PICTURES
HIGH DEFINITION CENTER

18

19
designer Earl Gee
design firm Gee + Chung Design
client IBM Software Station
Logo for an interactive kiosk which offers customers electronic delivery of software on-demand via satellite transmission.

20
designer Paul Weingartner
art directors Joan Hausman
Steve Turner
design firm Hausman Design
client Metricom, Inc.
Identity for a wireless communications company.

21
designers Paul Weingartner
Steve Turner
design firm Hausman Design
client Maxtor
Marks for a disk drive company.

22
designer Lynne Lukenbill
design firm Digital Typography & Design
client Data Marketing Inc.
Logo for a direct mail marketing firm.

23
designer Paul Weingartner
art directors Steve Turner
Joan Hausman
design firm Hausman Design
client Altera
Mark for a semi-conductor programming company.

SOFTWARE STATION™

19

20

21

22

D A T A   M A R K E T I N G   I N C.

23

24
designer John Ball
design firm Mires Design
client STAC
Logo for a software company.

25
designer Alexander Atkins
design firm Alexander Atkins Design, Inc.
client Alexander Atkins Design, Inc.
Logo for a graphic design studio.

26
designer Earl Gee
art director Fani Chung
design firm Gee + Chung Design
client Vitria Technology, Inc.
Logo for a high technology consulting firm providing information systems for large multinational corporations and government agencies.

27
designers Edoardo Chavarin
Larimie Garcia
design firm gig
client Innovation Snowboards
Logo for a snowboard manufacturer.

28
designer Larimie Garcia
design firm gig
client Swiss Jesus
Logo for a musical group.

24

25

26

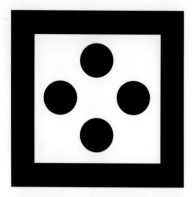

innovation
SNOWBOARDS

27

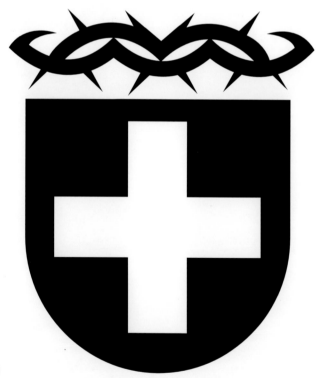

28

29
designer Glenn Martinez
design firm Glenn Martinez and Associates
client Stellar Ceramics
Logo for a ceramic tile
manufacturer.

30
designers Larry Vigon
Brian Jackson
design firm Vigon/Ellis
client Bridgwater Consulting Group
Logo for a technology
consulting group.

31
designers Larry Vigon
Marc Yeh
design firm Vigon/Ellis
client Century Housing Corporation
Logo for a low-income housing
financier and developer.

32
designer Daren L. Passolt
design firm Visualizer Design Studios
client Spectris
Badge logo created for Spectris
mainframe computers.

33
designers Larry Vigon
Marc Yeh
design firm Vigon/Ellis
client Day Info
Logo for an Australian
software company.

34
designer Steve Twigger
art director Rod Dyer
design firm Dyer/Mutchnick Group Inc.
client Logo for a cable TV Network that
runs infomercials.

29

30

31

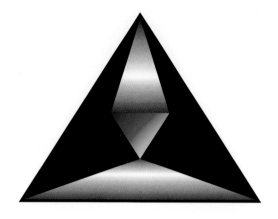

S P E C T R I S

32

D A Y   I N F O

33

PRODUCT
INFORMATION
NETWORK

34

35
designer   Cheryl Pelly
design firm   Designworks/USA
client   BMW NA
Logo for a worldwide BMW
conference for vendors held in
Tucson, Arizona.

36
designer   Darryl Glass
art director   Lauren Bruhn
design firm   Laura Coe Design Associates
client   John Schulz Photography
Logo for a corporate photographer.

37
designer   Glenn Martinez
design firm   Glenn Martinez and Associates
client   Sonoma County AIDS Memorial

38
designers   Larry Vigon
   Rowena Curtis
design firm   Vigon/Ellis
client   Can't Sing Can't Dance Productions
Logo for a television production
company.

39
designer   Martha Newton Furman
design firm   Martha Newton Furman Design &
   Illustration
client   Martha Newton Furman Design &
   Illustration
Logo for a design and illustration firm.

40
designer   Daren L. Passolt
design firm   Visualizer Design Studios
client   Visualizer Design Studios
Self-promotional logo/badge,
created for embroidered baseball
hats and T-Shirts.

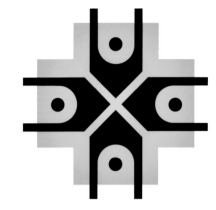

35

36

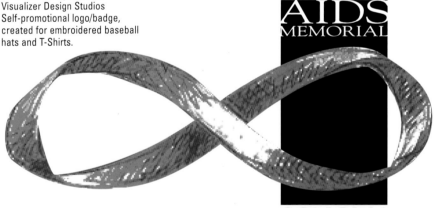

37   IN OUR HEARTS FOREVER

22

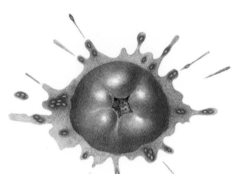

CAN'T SING CAN'T DANCE

38

PRODUCTIONS

39

40   v i s u a l i z e r

41
designer   Margo Chase
design firm Margo Chase Design
client   Kemper Snowboards
               Product identity for Kemper
               Snowboards.

42
designer   Julia Chong Tam
design firm Julia Tam Design
client   Milestones
               Logo for a greeting card company.

43
designer   Christopher Cantley
art director Rod Dyer
design firm Dyer/Mutchnick Group Inc.
client   New Star Pictures
               Logo for a motion picture
               production company.

44
designer   Edoardo Chavarin
design firm gig
               Logo for a non-profit organization
               for human rights at the border of
               Mexico and the United States.

45
designer   Steve Turner
art director Steve Turner
illustrator Jae Shim
design firm Hausman Design
client   California Water Service Company
               Identity for a water utility company.

41

42

43

44

45

46
designer   Cheryl Pelly
design firm   Pelly Design Associates
client   David A. Steputis, D.D.S.
               Logo for a dentist.

47
art director   Rod Dyer
design firm   Dyer/Mutchnick Group Inc.
client   Leo Burnett/Sony
               Retail logo for Sony Surround Sound.

48
designer   Laura Mische
art directors Linda Warren
               Monty House
design firm   Warren Group
client   Tektronix
               Logo for a global
               high-technology company.

49
designer   Mamoru Shimokochi
art director   Anne Reeves
design firm   Shimokochi/Reeves
client   UCLA
               Logo for the 50th anniversary of the school
               of theater, film and television at UCLA.

50
designer   Daren L. Passolt
design firm   Visualizer Design Studios
client   Manufacturing Education
               Logo created for manufacturing education
               service provider.

51
designers   Larry Vigon
               Brian Jackson
illustrator   Steve Berman
design firm   Vigon/Ellis
client   Rangers
               Logo for a die casting company.

David A. Steputis, D.D.S.

46

SONY MAXIMUM TELEVISION™

47

48

49

EDUCATION

50

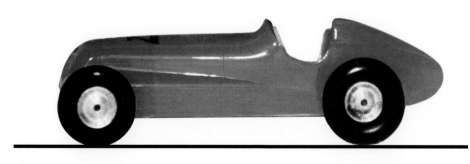

R A N G E R S

S I N C E 1 9 4 6

51

52
designers   Larry Vigon
          Brian Jackson
design firm Vigon/Ellis
client H_2O
          Logo for a water supply company
          for film studios.

53
designers   Larry Vigon
          Brian Jackson
design firm Vigon/Ellis
client   Sin-Drome Ltd.
          Logo for a record
          production company.

54
designer   Linda Kahn
art director Chip Clark
design firm Kahn Artist Design
client   Chip Clark Engineering

55
designer   Mark Kawakami
design firm M-Studios
client   Honda
          Logo for Honda's
          motorcycle division.

56
designer   John Ball
illustrator Miguel Perez
design firm Mires Design
client   McGraw Hill Home Interactive
          Logo for a CD Rom publisher.

57
designer   Mamoru Shimokochi
art director Anne Reeves
design firm Shimokochi/Reeves
client   X-Century
          Logo for a production studio
          in Japan.

58
designer   Jeff Kahn
art director Susan Tate
design firm Kahn Design
client   Revlon
          Logo for a botanical oil
          cosmetic product.

59
designer   Michael Stinson
design firm Stinson Design
client   Sinomex
          Logo for a Chinese owned business
          located in Mexico.

H
2

52

SIN·DROME
RECORDS LTᴰ

53

54

55

56

57

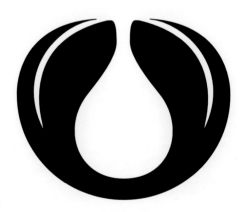

58

59

60
designer   Alexander Atkins
design firm Alexander Atkins Design, Inc.
client   Stanford Business School Alumni
            Association
            Logo for organization providing
            activities, services and benefits to
            alumni.

61
designer   Cheryl Pelly
design firm Pelly Design Associates
client   Las Calidas
            Logo for a Mexican resort.

62
designer   John White
illustrator Jerry Lofquist
design firm White Design, Inc.
client   National Physicians Network
            Logo for a multi-specialty
            medical group.

63
designer   Glenn Martinez
design firm Glenn Martinez and Associates
client   virtual HeadQuarters
            Logo for a software company.

**STANFORD
BUSINESS
SCHOOL
ALUMNI
ASSOCIATION**

60

61

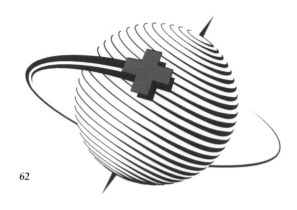

62

virtual HeadQuarters

63

64

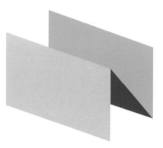

NOTEWORTHY

65

DisneyInteractive

66

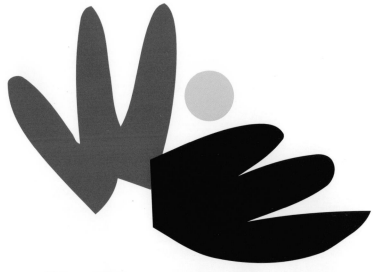

Together we're the best.
Los Angeles.

67

68
designers   Larry Vigon
               Brian Jackson
design firm Vigon/Ellis
client   Joint
               Logo for a Las Vegas resort.

69
designer   Diane Kuntz
design firm Diane Kuntz Design
client   Filmlink International
               Logo for a Japanese-American
               film venture.

70
designer   Sarah Tannas
design firm Tannas Design
client   Explore
               Proposed logo for a unisex clothing
               company specializing in outdoor
               active wear.

71
designer   Dana Lamb
design firm Sleepy Hollow Design
client   Water Warrior
               Logo for a line of toys.

72
designer   Sarah Tannas
design firm Tannas Design
client   The Learning Alliance
               Logo for an on-campus club
               that introduces Freshmen
               students to college.

68

69

70

71

72

73

designer	Ryoichi Yotsumoto
art director	Laura Coe Wright
design firm	Laura Coe Design Associates
client	Sport Sling
	Logo for soccer gear bags.

74

designer	Jann Bielenberg
illustrator	Eric David
design firm	Bielenberg Design Group
client	The Cassie Awards
	Logo for the telecast awards show for the casino/resort entertainment industry.

75

designer	Douglas Bogner
art directors	Syndine Imholte
	Joanne McGowen
design firm	Bullzye Design & Marketing
client	Aon Consulting Inc.
	Logo for an insurance and compensation brokerage company, consultants to businesses.

76

designer	Douglas Bogner
design firm	Bullzye Design & Marketing
client	The Tutoring Center
	Logo for a company's stationery, collateral and signage.

77

designer	Laurel Bigley Mathe
art director	Paul Page
illustrator	Laura Zugzda
design firm	Page Design, Inc.
client	Chocoholics Devine Desserts
	Logo for makers of chocolate sauce, chocolate pasta, etc.

73

74

75

76

77

78
designers	MaryAnn Mastrandrea
	Primo Angeli
art directors	Carlo Pagoda
	Richard Scheve
design firm	Primo Angeli Inc.
client	Beer Gear

Logo for a line of clothing for BrewMakers, a do-it-yourself beer brewery.

79
designer	Konrad Bright
design firm	Bright Strategic Design
client	Peter Miller Photography and Film

Logo for a still and motion picture photographer.

80
designer	Russell Leong
design firm	Russell Leong Design
client	Chris Brightman

Logo for a lighting designer and manufacturer.

81
designer	Russell Leong
illustrator	Mark Fox
design firm	Russell Leong Design
client	Worksmart Technologies

Logo for a new class of PC-based software that automates routine tasks associated with the retrieval and delivery of information.

82
designer	Jon Lagda
art director	Ron Scheibel
design firm	Hunt, Rook & Scheibel
client	SSE Foods Inc.

Proposed logo for a frozen food manufacturer.

83
designer	Peter Nam
design firm	Peter Nam Design
client	Taste Vacations

Logo for a line of exotic condiments.

78

79

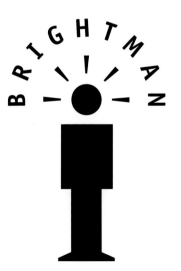

80

81

82

83

84
designer   Diane Kuntz
design firm   Diane Kuntz Design
client   An Evening in Rio
Logo for a fund-raising event for a
local hospital.

85
designer   Jim Wylie
design firm   B-Square
client   Southern Gourmet Cookie Company
Logo for a small gourmet cookie
company.

86
designer   Paul Morales
design firm   Onyx Design Inc.
client   Birkenstock
Logo for back-to-school
shoes and sandals.

87
designer   Miles Beller
design firm   Beller Design
client   Homefront Broadcasting
Logo for an internet start-up
company looking to bring radio
transmissions to the net.

88
designer   Paul Morales
design firm   Onyx Design Inc.
client   La Raza Centro Legao, Inc.
Logo for a social service law
agency's fund-raising dinner.

89
designer   Laurel Bigley Mathe
art director   Paul Page
design firm   Page Design, Inc.
client   Tasty Pockets
Logo for a manufacturer of
food products.

84

85

86

87

HOMEFRONT BROADCASTING

88

89

90
designer   Howard Ian Schiller
design firm   Designwise
client   Mobile Video
Logo for a video rental store.

91
designer   Konrad Bright
design firm   Bright Strategic Design
client   Lopez Electric
Logo for an electrical contractor.

92
designer   Barbara Brown
design firm   Barbara Brown Marketing and
   Design
client   Ventura County Medical Resource
   Foundation
Logo for a foundation that provides
medical and financial support for
the local medical community.

93
designer   Debbie Smith
art director   David Leong
design firm   Addis Group
client   Holland Brothers
Logo for a manufacturer of quality-
crafted leather goods.

94
designer   Ray Wood
art director   Keith Bright
design firm   Bright Strategic Design
client   Wok Fast
Logo for a fast food
Chinese restaurant.

95
designer   Diane Kuntz
design firm   Diane Kuntz Design
client   CREST
Logo for a citywide childcare/
afterschool program.

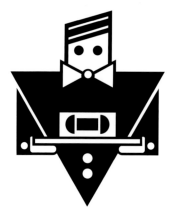

90

91

92

H O L L A N D

B R O T H E R S™

H A N D M A D E   I N   A M E R I C A

93

WOK FAST

94

95

96
designer   Diane Kuntz
dillustrator   April Bryant
design firm   Diane Kuntz Design
client   California Hospital Medical Center
                Logo for the medical center.

97
designer   Diane Kuntz
dillustrator   Linda Eberle
design firm   Diane Kuntz Design
client   Grand Hope Neonatology
                Group Inc.
                Logo for the NICU unit at California
                Hospital Medical Center.

98
designer   Kimberly Lentz Powell
art director   Doug Akagi
design firm   Akagi Remington
client   Janice Tomita P.T. and Associates
                Logo for a physical therapist.

99
designer   Konrad Bright
design firm   Bright Strategic Design
client   Moffit Productions
                Logo for a line of videos on
                swimming.

100
designer   Jane McCambell
art director   Doug Akagi
design firm   Akagi Remington
client   Paul Margolies
                Logo for a photographer.

101
designer   Becca Smidt
design firm   Becca Smidt
client   Maitri Aids Hospice
                Logo for a home for people
                with Aids.

96

97

98

99

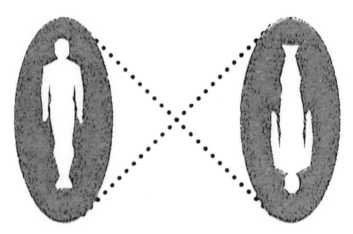

100

101

102
designer   Jeni Olsen
art director Nancy Daniels
design firm The GNU Group
client   Muju Resort
Logo for one of various Muju
resorts in Korea.

103
designer   Jeni Olsen
art director Nancy Daniels
design firm The GNU Group
client   Muju Resort
Logo for one of various Muju
resorts in Korea.

104
designer   Jeni Olsen
art director Nancy Daniels
design firm The GNU Group
client   Muju Resort
Logo for one of various Muju
resorts in Korea.

105
designer   Paul Weingartner
design firm pw Design
client   Second Harvest Food Bank
Logo for a non-profit food bank for
families in need.

106
designer   Brad Maur
design firm Page Design, Inc.
client   Corporate Learning Center
Logo for an educational division of
the Money Store.

107
designer   Rod Dyer
illustrator Andy Engel
design firm Dyer/Mutchnick Group Inc.
client   Maverick
Logo for an entertainment
company.

102

103

104

105

106

107

108
designer   Brad Maur
design firm   Page Design, Inc.
client   Reebock
             Logo for a manufacturer of outdoor
             footwear and clothing.

109
designer   Qris Yamashita
art director Rod Dyer
design firm   Dyer/Mutchnick Group Inc.
client   Pivot Tour
             Logo for a tour
             organizer/travel agency.

110
designers   Larry Vigon
             Brian Jackson
illustrator   Julie Dennis
design firm   Vigon/Ellis
client   Friedland Jacobs Communications
             Logo for an entertainment
             advertising agency.

111
designer   Mike Brower
design firm   Mires Design
client   Bod-e
             Logo for a personal health and
             fitness trainer.

112
designer   Jon Lagda
design firm   K3 Kato Kreative Koncepts
client   CSULB Performing Arts Center
             Logo for a performing arts center.

113
designer   Jeff Kahn
design firm   Kahn Design
client   Puddle Dancer Press
             Logo for a publisher of
             inspirational, spiritual and
             recovery-oriented books.

114
designers   Larry Vigon
             Brian Jackson
design firm   Vigon/Ellis
client   The Mad Platter
             Logo for a caterer.

108

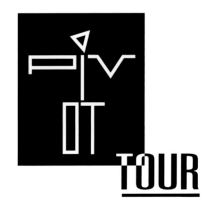

109

110

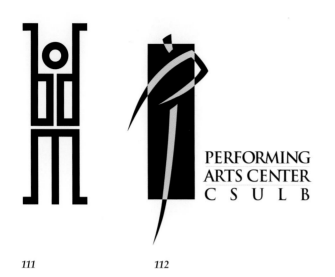

PERFORMING
ARTS CENTER
C S U L B

PuddleDancer PRESS ™

111   112   113

THE MAD PLATTER

114

C A T E R I N G · S P E C I A L   E V E N T S

115
designer Peter Sargent
art director Greg Berman
design firm Sargent & Berman
client BoyerSports
Logo for an importer of fine cycling accessories.

116
designer Glenn Sakamoto
art director Rod Dyer
design firm Dyer/Mutchnick Group Inc.
client Talent Entertainment Management
Logo for the company creates a "human" manager.

117
designer Linda Kahn
art director Micki Wilson
design firm Frank Templeton Inc.
client Micki Wilson/Franklin Templeton Inc.
Logo for innovative software to speed up common tasks.

118
designer Hun Wynn
art director Rod Dyer
design firm Dyer/Mutchnick Group Inc.
client By Storm Entertainment
Logo for a music label.

119
designer William Kent
art director Tricia Rauen
design firm Buz Design Group
client Adelson Entertainment
Logo for entertainment productions.

BOYERSPORTS

115

TALENT ENTERTAINMENT MANAGEMENT

116

117

118 BY STORM™ ENTERTAINMENT

119 **adelson** entertainment

120
designers Larry Vigon
Brian Jackson
design firm Vigon/Ellis
client Zoë
Logo for a Pilates exercise studio.

121
designer Steven Morris
design firm Steven Morris Design
client Harvest Earth Fair
Logo for a festival for
environmentalism.

122
designer Larry Vigon
illustrator Marc Yeh
design firm Vigon/Ellis
client Max
Logo for an online
production resource.

123
designer Rod Dyer
design firm Dyer/Mutchnick Group Inc.
client Rooster Entertainment Group
Logo for promoting the fun and
romance of studying abroad.

120

121

122

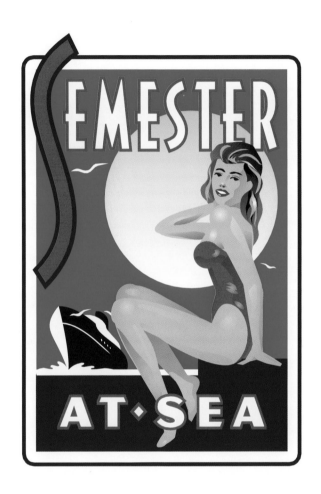

123

124
designers   Marcelo De Freitas
           Primo Angeli
art director Carlo Pagoda
design firm Primo Angeli Inc.
client   San Francisco Film Society
           Logo for the San Francisco
           International Film Festival.

125
designer   Michael Stinson
design firm Kelston International, Inc.
client   Centor
           Logo for manufacturer and
           producer of CD Rom database
           software for optimum retrieval.

126
designer   Michael Stinson
design firm Kelston International, Inc.
client   Centor
           Logo for a manufacturer and
           producer of CD Rom database
           software for optimum retrieval.

127
designer   Mamoru Shimokochi
art director Anne Reeves
design firm Shimokochi/Reeves
client   S/R Marketing Man
           Logo for identity and package
           design consultants.

124

125

126

127

™

128
designer John Smeaton
art director Scott A. Mednick
design firm Think New Ideas
client ECO Halloween Bash
Logo for an environmental
group in Hollywood..

129
designer José A. Serrano
illustrator Tracy Sabin
design firm Mires Design
client Nike
Logo for Nike, Deion Sanders
cross-training shoes.

130
designer Michael Stinson
design firm Stinson Design
client Autokickers!
Logo for an adolescent
paintball team.

131
designer Julie Ann Stricklin
design firm The Stricklin Companies
client Nickel Slick
Logo for a rock and roll band.

132
designer Lissa Patrizi
design firm Patrizi Designs
client The Wright Touch
Logo for decorative painting and
architectural painting and finishes.

133
designer Deborah Hom
art director José A. Serrano
illustrator Tracy Sabin
design firm Mires Design
client Industry Pictures
Logo for a motion picture
company.

128

129

130

131

132

133

134
designer   Daren L. Passolt
design firm Visualizer Design Studios
client   Raymac
            Logo created for custom made
            bicycle frames.

135
designer   Larimie Garcia
design firm gig
client   Sin Sity
            Logo for an adult video and
            accessory store.

136
designer   Jefrey Gunion
design firm Jefrey Gunion Illustration & Design
client   The Electric Library
            Logo for an online "library" service
            with powerful search engine.

137
designer   Arne Ratermanis
design firm Arne Ratermanis
client   One Singles Club
            Logo for a singles club.

138
designer   Arne Ratermanis
design firm Lorenz Advertising & Design, Inc.
client   CST Images
            Logo for a software developer
            specializing in programs that
            reduce software development time.

139
designer   Laurel Bigley Mathe
art director Paul Page
illustrator Laura Zugzda
design firm Page Design, Inc.
client   Harlow's
            Logo for an Italian restaurant with a
            1930s theme.

140
designer   Alexander Atkins
design firm Alexander Atkins Design, Inc.
client   Lindstrom Represents
            Logo for company
            representing artists.

134

135

136

SINGLES CLUB

137

CST Images

™

138

MODERN ITALIAN

139

140

141
designers   Larry Vigon
             Brian Jackson
illustrator Denise Milford
design firm Vigon/Ellis
client   Clive Wilkinson Architecture
             Logo for an architect.

142
designer   Martha Newton Furman
design firm Martha Newton Furman
             Design & Illustration
client   Martha Newton Furman Design &
             Illustration
             Icon created to promote the
             designer/illustrator.

143
designer   Mark Allen
art director Trish Burke
design firm Mark Allen Design
client   Dumb & Dumber
             Logo for Dumb & Dumber
             TV show merchandise.

144
designer   Mike Salisbury
illustrator Dave Willardson
design firm Mike Salisbury
             Communications, Inc.
client   Powerhouse
             Logo for a full service,
             state-of-the-art digital and
             conventional service bureau.

145
designer   Brad Maur
design firm Page Design, Inc.
client   Reebok
             Logo for an outdoor footwear and
             clothing manufacturer.

146
designers   Mark Jones
              Terrence Tong
art directors Carlo Pagoda
              Nina Dietzel
design firm   Primo Angeli Inc.
client   Noah's Bagels
              Logo for bagel outlets.

141

142

143

144

145

146

147
designer Jeff Ivarson
design firm Ivarson Design Group
client Roughneck
Logo for a manufacturer of
fishing rods.

148
designer Jefrey Gunion
design firm Jefrey Gunion Illustration & Design
client Advanced Communications Group
Logo for a high level
communication techniques training
and consultation group.

149
designer John Smeaton
art director Scott A. Mednick
design firm Think New Ideas
client Guys Tuys
Logo for a manufacturer of
designer ties.

150
designer Daren L. Passolt
design firm Visualizer Design Studios
client American Cyclist
Logo for custom made bicycle
frames and components.

151
designer Rose Hartono
art director Tricia Rauen
design firm Buz Design Group
client Node Warrior Networks
Logo for an internet server.

147

148

149

150

151

152
designer	Qris Yamashita
art director	Rod Dyer
design firm	Dyer/Mutchnick Group Inc.
client	J B Music Publishing LLC
	Logo for a hip music publishing company.

153
designer	Alexander Atkins
design firm	Alexander Atkins Design, Inc.
client	Abbott Usability
	Logo for company conducting product evaluations.

154
designer	Mark Kawakami
design firm	M-Studios
client	Quiksilver Eyewear
	Logo for a manufacturer of sunglasses.

155
designer	Jeff Yeh
art director	Ron Scheibel
design firm	Hunt, Rook & Scheibel
client	Hunt, Rook & Scheibel
	Logo for an advertising agency.

156
designers	Doug Akagi
	Lorsen Koo
art director	Doug Akagi
design firm	Akagi Remington
client	Freestyle
	Logo for a fast food franchise.

152

153

154

155

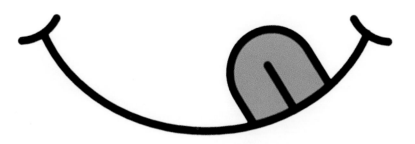

156

157
designer   Paul Weingartner
design firm   pw Design
client   Allen Hadley, CMT
          Logo for a personal masseur.

158
designer   Paul Weingartner
design firm   pw Design
client   Castro Village Pharmacy
          Logo for a pharmacy.

159
designer   Bill Kent
art director   Tricia Rauen
design firm   Buz Design Group
client   Adelson Entertainment
          Logo for entertainment
          productions.

160
designer   Jeanine Colini
illustrator   Patsy Tucker
design firm   Jeanine Colini Design Associates
client   Training With Tambourine
          Logo for animal behavioral
          specialists.

161
designer   Darlene McElroy
design firm   Darlene McElroy Design
client   Karen McKee
          Logo for an art therapist.

157

158

159

160

KAREN·McKEE

Art Therapist

161

162
designer | Ray Wood
art director | Keith Bright
design firm | Bright Strategic Design
client | South Park Sports Stadium Group
Logo for a sports group formed to bring a new state-of-the-art football stadium to Los Angeles.

163
designer | Konrad Bright
design firm | Bright Strategic Design
client | Danny Sullivan Inc.
Logo for a race car company.

164
designer | Julia Chong Tam
design firm | Julia Tam Design
client | SBJT
Logo for a youth tennis league.

165
designer | Dana Lamb
design firm | Sleepy Hollow Design
client | Chino Unified School District
Pro-bono logo for a children's athletic competition to raise money for art programs.

166
designer | Ryoichi Yotsumoto
art director | Laura Coe Wright
design firm | Laura Coe Design Associates
client | The Active Foot
Logo for direct mail running shoe sales.

167
designers | José Serrano
 | Mark Mattingly
illustrator | Mark Mattingly
design firm | Mires Design
client | Hage Elementary
Logo for a promotional T-shirt given away to children who belonged to the school's chess club.

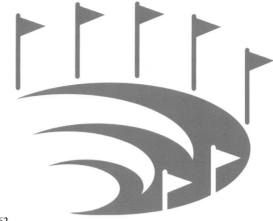

162

163

164

165

166

167

168
designer   Daren L. Passolt
design firm   Visualizer Design Studios
client   Stanford University/Amdahl
Corporation
Created for an educational InRoads
Challenge Program, sponsored
by Amdahl Corporation and
Stanford University.

169
designer   Vicki Wyatt
art director   Patti Judd
design firm   Juddesign
client   Sun 'n' Sand
Logo for a volleyball sportswear
manufacturer.

170
designer   José A. Serrano
art director   Miguel Perez
illustrator   Carl Vanderschuit
design firm   Mires Design
client   Voit Sports
Logo for a project to introduce a
brand new line of ball with a
unique grip.

171
designer   Bradley W. Grose
design firm   Bradley Grose Design
client   Pasadena Rose Bowl
Logo for the World Cup
opening ceremony.

172
designer   Scott Mires
illustrator   Tracy Sabin
design firm   Mires Design
client   LA Gear
Logo for a footwear product line.

173
designers   Miguel Perez
Scott Mires
design firm   Mires Design
client   Nike
Logo for Michael Jordon's
retirement celebration.

168

sun 'n' sand

169

170

171

172

173

174
designer Cheryl Gillis
art directors Greg Berman
Peter Sargent
design firm Princess Cruises
client L.A. Care Health Plan
Logo for the cruise ship
Dawn Princess.

175
designer Carol Gravelle
art directors Carol Gravelle
David Wood
design firm Carol Gravelle Graphic Design
client Xircom
Logo for sales incentive program
for networking products.

176
designer Julia Chong Tam
design firm Julia Tam Design
client Hellenic American Cruises
Logo for a cruise ship of
two countries.

177
designer Peter Sargent
art director Greg Berman
design firm Sargent & Berman
client Breaking Away
Logo for a bicycle touring company.

178
designer Riki Komachi
design firm Riki Komachi
client Bikes For Cops
Logo for joint effort of Venice police
and sheriff to buy more bikes for
patrol.

174

175

HELLENIC AMERICAN
CRUISES

176

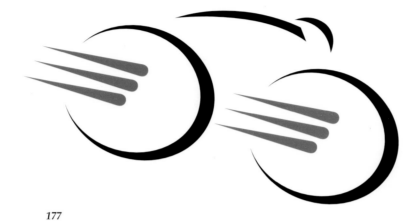

177

178

179
designer   Bradley W. Grose
art director   Charlie Shaw
design firm   Bradley Grose Design
client   Pat Boone
             Logo for a poster commemorating
             the 40th anniversary of Pat Boone's
             first million-selling song, "Ain't
             That a Shame."

180
designer   Bradley W. Grose
design firm   Bradley Grose Design
client   Hughes Aircraft Corporation
             Logo for Naval Air Weapons
             Command counter measures
             receiving set.

181
designer   Bradley W. Grose
art director   Tim Ramos
design firm   Bradley Grose Design
client   Disney Home Video
             New packaging logo for Vintage
             Disney Cartoon Classics.

182
designer   Bradley W. Grose
design firm   Bradley Grose Design
             Logo for WWII ace Colonel
             Herschel H. Green.

183
designer   Bradley W. Grose
design firm   Bradley Grose Design
client   Edwards Air Force Base, Southern
             California
             Logo for the 50th anniversary of
             America's first jet flight.

184
designer   Bradley W. Grose
design firm   Bradley Grose Design
client   United States Navy/Jet Pioneers of
             the U.S.A.
             Logo for the U.S. Navy's 50th
             anniversary of the first jet propelled
             carrier take-off and landing.

179

180

181

182

183

184

185
art director   Tricia Rauen
design firm   Buz Design Group
client   Rockwell Federal Credit Union
Logo for a kids' banking program.

186
art director   Tricia Rauen
design firm   Buz Design Group
client   Rockwell Federal Credit Union
Logo for a kids' banking program.

187
designer   Laurel Bigley Mathe
art director   Paul Page
design firm   Page Design, Inc.

188
designer   Barbara D. Cummings
art director   David Parker
design firm   DAA
client   Caribbean Traders
Logo for retailers of adventurous
lifestyle gear.

189
designer   Michael Ketz
illustrator   Jennifer Hewitson
design firm   Hetz Advertising & Design
client   Ark Enterprises
Logo for a marketing and public
relations firm.

190
designer   Dana Lamb
art director   Steve Forbes
design firm   Sleepy Hollow Design
client   Ingram-Micro, Inc.
Logo for an Ingram-Micro
promotional campaign for Apple
Macintosh product line.

185

186

187

188

189

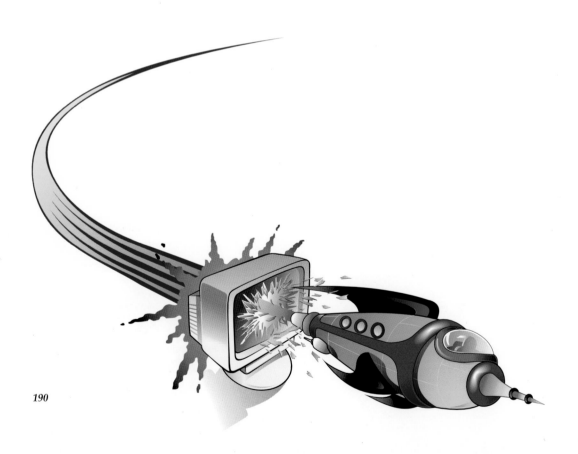

190

191
designer   Jay Galster
art director   Jerry Takigawa
design firm   Jerry Takigawa Design
client   ColorAd Printers
Logo for a printer.

192
designer   Gregory Thomas
design firm   Gregory Thomas Associates
client   Monarch Pictures
Logo for a division of Tristar
Pictures.

193
designer   Martha Newton Furman
design firm   Martha Newton Furman Design &
Illustration
client   Martha Newton Furman Design &
Illustration
Logo for a holiday greeting card.

194
designer   Margo Chase
design firm   Margo Chase Design
client   Kemper Snowboards
Product identity for Kemper
Snowboards.

195
designer   Ryoichi Yotsumoto
art director   Laura Coe Wright
design firm   Laura Coe Design Associates
client   Peregrine Solutions
Logo for a law firm that specializes
in legal defense cost management.

196
designer   Ray Wood
design firm   Bright Strategic Design
client   NATPE
Logo for a professional association
of television producers and
executives.

191

192

193

194

195

196

197-201
designer   Corinne Char
art director   Nancy Daniels
design firm   The GNU Group
client   Deer Valley Center
             Logos for a neighborhood shopping
             center in Phoenix, Arizona.

197

198

199

200

201

202
designer Jon Lagda
art director Ron Scheibel
design firm Hunt, Rook & Scheibel
client Roosters
Proposed logo for a distributor of
frozen breakfast entrees.

203
designer Jeff Yeh
art director Ron Scheibel
design firm Hunt, Rook & Scheibel
client Cock-A-Doodle Doos
Logo for a maker of breakfast
food items.

204
designer Sarah Tannas
art director Ron Scheibel
design firm Hunt, Rook & Scheibel
client Coyote Grill
Proposed logo for a line of
Southwestern entrees.

205
designer Jeanine Colini
illustrator Jeanine Colini
design firm Jeanine Colini Design Associates
client Greater Los Angeles Zoo
Association
Logo for an annual fund raising
benefit for the Los Angeles Zoo.

206
designer Jeanine Colini
illustrator Jeanine Colini
design firm Jeanine Colini Design Associates
client Colini + Company
Logo for the sale and promotion of
the "A to Zoo" poster which
consists of 26 illustrated animal
characters.

202

203

204

205

206

207
designer Carol Gravelle
art directors Carol Gravelle
Barbara Mizuno
design firm Mizuno & Associates
client Weider
Logo for bodybuilding and
fitness products.

208
designer Barbara Brown
design firm Barbara Brown Marketing and
Design
client Spot Satellite
Logo intended to communicate
company's desire to "sit up,
roll over and fetch."

209
designer Gerald Reis
illustrator Susan Greinetz
design firm Gerald Reis Design Studio
client Lindsay Wildlife Museum
Logo for a museum committed to
the welfare of the natural world.

210
designer Kimberly Lentz Powell
art director Doug Akagi
design firm Akagi Remington
client Sun Fun
Logo for children's and maternity
clothing stores

211
designer Glenn Martinez
design firm Glenn Martinez and Associates
client Avalon Natural Cosmetics
Logo for a health and beauty
products company.

212
designer Glenn Martinez
design firm Glenn Martinez and Associates
client American Red Cross
Logo for a fashion show and
auction to benefit Red Cross.

207

208

209

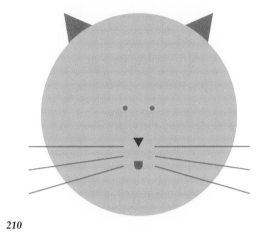

210

211

212

213
designer   Dana Lamb
design firm   Sleepy Hollow Design
client   Bikini Shark
Logo for start-up company
for beachwear.

214
designer   Mary Anne Mastandrea
design firm   Mastandrea Design
client   Marine Mammal Center
Logo for the Marine Mammal
Center's 20th anniversary.

215
designer   Carol Gravelle
art directors   Carol Gravelle
Barbara Mizuno
design firm   Mizuno & Associates
client   Innovation Sports
Logo showing durability and
toughness of bike trailers.

216
designer   Miguel Perez
design firm   Mires Design
client   AlliKat Records and Cafe
Logo for a record store with a
coffee shop.

217
designer   Diane Kuntz
art director   Marnell Jameson
design firm   Diane Kuntz Design
client   Hidden Valley Ranch
Logo for a working ranch in
Calabasas that breeds race horses.

218
designer   Ron Miriello
illustrator   Tracy Sabin
design firm   Miriello Grafico, Inc.
client   Browndeer Press
Logo for a children's book
publisher.

213

214

215

216

217

BROWNDEER
PRESS

218

219
designer	Mary Anne Mastandrea
art director	Elizabeth Keenan
design firm	Studio 77/Goldberg Moser O'Neill
client	Heavenly Ski Resort
	Logo for the ski resort's cantina

220
designer	Michael Ketz
illustrator	Laura Jose
design firm	Hetz Advertising & Design
client	Pelican Ridge
	Logo for a real estate housing development.

221
designer	Laurel Bigley Mathe
art director	Paul Page
design firm	Page Design, Inc.
client	NorthBay Healthcare System
	Logo created to promote an event for anyone who had been born at NorthBay Hospital.

222
designer	Cheryl Pelly
design firm	Pelly Design Associates
client	Indigo Iguana
	Logo for a restaurant/cantina.

223
designers	Larry Vigon
	Brian Jackson
illustrator	Daniel and Louise Schriede
design firm	Vigon/Ellis
client	Robin Sloan
	Logo for Robin Sloan's home.

224
designer	Russell Leong
illustrator	Sandy Gin
design firm	Russell Leong Design
client	Radical Concepts
	Logo for custom beanbag chair designers and manufacturers.

219

220

221

222

223   *R o b i n   S l o a n*

224

225
designer   Mark Kawakami
design firm M-Studios
client   Dog Eat Dog Apparel
           Logo for a clothing manufacturer.

226
designer   Zion Wu-Yip
art director Jeff Ivarson
illustrator Filip Yip
design firm Ivarson Design Group
client   California Graphics, Inc.
           Logo for a one-stop digital pre-
           press service bureau.

227
designers Laura Greer
           Darryl Glass
art director Lauren Bruhn
illustrator Ryoichi Yotsumoto
design firm Laura Coe Design Associates
client   Titleist and Foot-Joy Worldwide
           Logo for a line of kids' golf clubs.

228
designers Larry Vigon
           Brian Jackson
illustrator Julie Dennis
design firm Vigon/Ellis
client   Total Multimedia
           Logo for a fractal compression
           technology company.

229
designers Ray Wood
           Sabine Desmond
design firm Bright Strategic Design
client   Mandalay Pictures
           Logo for a movie and
           entertainment company.

225

California Graphics, Inc.

226

227

T O T A L

MULTIMEDIA

228

229

230
designer Jeff Heesch
art director Michael Stinson
design firm Stinson Design
client Viking Star Enterprise
Logo for a business consultant.

231
designer Glenn Martinez
design firm Glenn Martinez and Associates
client Enchanté
Logo for a producer of books,
videos and films geared at boosting
children's self-esteem.

232
designer Jeni Olsen
art director Nancy Daniels
design firm The GNU Group
client Lorin
Logo for a hotel based in Indonesia.

233
designer Daren L. Passolt
design firm Visualizer Design Studios
client The Fly
Created for a boys' and men's
fishing event.

234
designer José A. Serrano
illustrator Tracy Sabin
design firm Mires Design
client Chaos Lures
Logo for fishing lures.

230

231

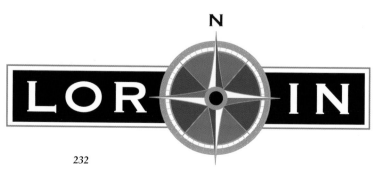

232

233

234

235
designer Jann Bielenberg
design firm Bielenberg Design Group
client Shores Financial
Logo for financial planning
services.

236
designer Steven Morris
design firm Steven Morris Design
client Lolo Company
Logo for toy, gift and game makers.

237
designer Miguel Perez
art director John Ball
illustrator Tracy Sabin
design firm Mires Design
client Rubio's Restaurants
Logo for a low-fat Mexican menu.

238
designer John Ball
illustrator Tracy Sabin
design firm Mires Design
client S.D. Johnson Co.
Logo for a line of fishing products.

239
designer Margo Chase
design firm Margo Chase Design
client Alternative Pick Creative Directory
Section title for "The Alternative
Pick," a creative talent sourcebook
for the music and entertainment
industries.

235

236

LOLO

COMPANY.©

237

238

239

240
designer   Glenn Sakamoto
art director Rod Dyer
design firm   Dyer/Mutchnick Group Inc.
client   Farrier's Nature
              Logo for company's environmental
              television personality.

241
designer   Dickson A. Keyser
design firm   Design Services of Dickson A.
              Keyser
client   Java Mania
              Logo for a coffee house.

242
designer   Bradley W. Grose
design firm   Bradley Grose Design
client   International Church of the
              Foursquare Gospel
              Logo for a gospel record company.

243
designers   Larry Vigon
              Brian Jackson
design firm   Vigon/Ellis
client   Headspace
              Logo for a multimedia music
              provider.

244
designers   Larry Vigon
              Brian Jackson
design firm   Vigon/Ellis
client   E2
              Logo for an environmental
              education program used in the
              Los Angeles school system.

245
designers   Larry Vigon
              Marc Yeh
design firm   Vigon/Ellis
client   Baldwin Productionsn
              Logo for a film production
              company.

240

241

242

HEADSPACE

243

E2
ENVIRONMENT
EDUCATION

244

BALDWIN
PRODUCTIONS

245

246
designer   Barbara D. Cummings
art director   David Parker
design firm   B.D. Cummings/Illustration
client   Vino Desert Classic
Logo for a golf tournament.

247
designer   Lisa Capriotti
design firm   Shurtz/Capriotti
client   Villa Italia
Logo for importer and distributor of
fine wines, predominately Italian.

248
designers   Dickson A. Keyser
    Mike Cotsifas
design firm   Cotsifas/Keyser Design Services
client   Bay Area Wine Storage
Logo for the custom storage of
collectable wine.

249
designer   Anna Wong
design firm   Akagi Remington
client   Sonoma County Harvest Fair
Logo for region's harvest,
showcasing wine, food and crafts.

250
designer   Joyce Sun
art directors   Greg Berman
    Peter Sargent
design firm   Sargent & Berman
client   Cystic Fibrosis
Logo for a fund-raising event
benefiting Cystic Fibrosis.

246

247

248

249

A Culinary Evening
with the California
Winemasters
BENEFITING CYSTIC FIBROSIS

250

ALADDIN

251

251
designer   Glenn Martinez
design firm Glenn Martinez and Associates
client   Aladdin Mortgage
                 Logo for a mortgage broker.

252
designer   Alexander Atkins
design firm Alexander Atkins Design, Inc.
client   Skinny Sippin
                 Logo for upscale fruit juice retailer.

253
designer   Michael Ketz
illustrator   Fiona King
design firm Hetz Advertising & Design
client   Fairway Oaks
                 Logo for a real estate housing
                 development.

254
designers   Dorothy Remington
                 Karin Myint
design firm Akagi Remington
client   Emily Sagar
                 Logo for a caterer and private chef.

252

253

254

255
designer Rod Dyer
design firm Dyer/Mutchnick Group Inc.
client Cheers London Bar & Grill
Logo for this bar is directly related
to the one in the television series.
This is an adaptation of the original
Cheers logo.

256
designer Arne Ratermanis
design firm Lorenz Advertising & Design, Inc.
client Golden Strand Pasta
Logo for a line of pasta products.

257
designers Rod Dyer
Terry Song
design firm Dyer/Mutchnick Group Inc.
client Sandro's Ciabatta
Logo for a traditional Italian bakery.

258
designer Steve Twigger
art director Rod Dyer
design firm Dyer/Mutchnick Group Inc.
client Shorty's Diner
Logo for Bruce Willis's restaurant
in Haley, Idaho.

255

256

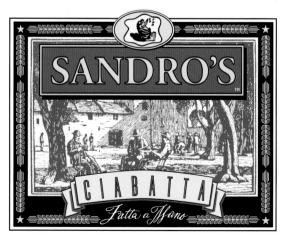

257

258

259
designer | Michael Ketz
illustrator | Dasha Jensen
design firm | Hetz Advertising & Design
client | Pizza Nova
Logo for a restaurant.

260
designer | Mary Anne Mastandrea
art director | Elizabeth Keenan
design firm | Studio 77/Goldberg Moser O'Neill
client | Heavenly Ski Resort
Logo for the ski resort's restaurant.

261
designers | Mike Brower
| Scott Mires
illustrator | Tracy Sabin
design firm | Mires Design
client | Food Group
Logo for a Boyd's Coffee promotion.

262
designers | Scott Mires
| Miguel Perez
art director | John Ball
design firm | Mires Design
client | Taco Pronto
Logo for a Mexican fast-food restaurant.

259

260

261

262

263
designer   Russell Leong
illustrator   Chad Kubo
design firm   Russell Leong Design
client   Roti
Logo for a rotisserie and grill
restaurant.

264
designer   Lewis Harrison
design firm   Lewis Harrison Design, Inc.
client   California Produce
Logo for a wholesale produce
company marketing to restaurants.

265
designer   Suzanne Bastear
illustrator   Janet Hekking
design firm   Armstrong Associates
client   Sonoma Food & Wine Classic
Logo for a regional gourmet food
and fine wine event.

266
designer   Cheri Knoy
art director   Karina Lorenz
design firm   Lorenz Advertising & Design, Inc.
client   Topit
Logo for a product which is a plant
growth regulator.

267
designer   Jeff Samaripa
design firm   Mires Design
client   Del Mar County Fair
Logo contest entry for
Del Mar County Fair.

263

264

265 SONOMA FOOD AND WINE CLASSIC

266

267

268
designer	Becca Smidt
art director	Sam Smidt
design firm	Sam Smidt Inc.
client	Spectrum Eye Physicians
	Logo for an eye care business.

269
designer	Howie Idelson
design firm	Urban Image Studio
client	Speed King Racing

270
designer	Konrad Bright
design firm	Bright Strategic Design
client	Panik Productions
	Logo for a film director.

271
designer	Russell Leong
design firm	Russell Leong Design
client	Programmers Press
	Logo for a publisher of computer books.

272
designer	Peter Sargent
art director	Greg Berman
design firm	Sargent & Berman
client	Toolbox
	Logo for a special effects and animation company.

273
designer	Darlene McElroy
design firm	Darlene McElroy Design
client	Four Women Artists
	Logo for four women artists who promote themselves as a team and have shows together.

274
designer	Jeff Kahn
design firm	Kahn Design
client	The Comedy Coach
	Logo for stand-up comedy trainer Neil Leiberman, San Francisco.

268

269

270

271

272

273

274

275
designer	Riki Komachi
design firm	Riki Komachi
client	Architects for Shelter
	Logo for the playhouse project.

276
designer	Greg Lindy
art directors	Jeri Heiden
	Michael Rey
design firm	Rey International
client	Warner Bros. Archives
	Logo for the recording company's classic recordings, reissues and compilations.

277
designer	Ray Marshall
design firm	Ray Marshall Design
client	John Murray Productions
	Logo for an event design and production company.

278
designer	Mark Allen
art director	Scott Pryor
design firm	Mark Allen Design
client	Borders Books
	Logos for Borders Book advertisements.

279
designer	Bill Corridori
art director	Keith Bright
design firm	Bright Strategic Design
client	Teenage Website
	Logo for the world's first online fan magazine.

280
designers	Leo Terrazas
	Daniel Ko
art director	Kathy Kirata
illustrator	Karen Nakatani
design firm	Patrick SooHoo Designers
client	L.A. Care Health Plan
	Logo for a health care plan to serve Medi-Cal beneficiaries in Los Angeles County.

275

276

277

278

279

280

281
designer Becca Smidt
art director Sam Smidt
design firm Sam Smidt, Inc.
client Women's Community Medical Center
Logo for a friendly, safe and private community medical center for women.

282
designer Han Vu
art director Jeffrey Shurtz
design firm Shurtz/Capriotti
client Sybase Worldwide Customer Support & Services
Logo for a database software company

283
designer Christine Cava
client Log On America
Logo for an online internet service.

284
designer Gale Spitzley
art director José A. Serrano
illustrator Dan Thoner
design firm Mires Design
client Pannikin
Logo for a 25th Anniversary promotion.

285
designer Deborah Hom
art director John Ball
design firm Mires Design
client Fusion Media
Logo for a multimedia developer.

286
designer Dickson A. Keyser
design firm Design Services of Dickson A. Keyser
client Self Identity
Logo for designer who specializes in solving people's identity problems.

287
designers Steve Turner
Paul Weingartner
art director Joan Hausman
design firm Hausman Design
client Meris Laboratories, Inc.
Logo for a testing laboratory.

281

282

283

284

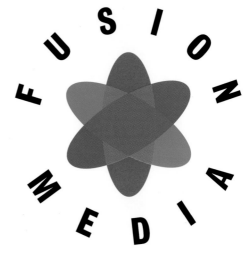

285

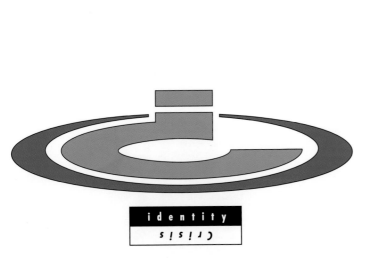

286

287 MERIS

288
designer Mario Porto
art director Lisa Capriotti
design firm Shurtz/Capriotti
client Made to Order Memories
Logo for upscale custom made gifts.

289
designer Han Vu
art director Jeffrey Shurtz
design firm Shurtz/Capriotti
client Sybase Training Program
Logo for a database software company.

290
designer Shelly Weir-Martinez
art director Jeffrey Shurtz
design firm Shurtz/Capriotti
client San Francisco Youth At Risk
Logo for a non-profit organization that helps disadvantaged children get education and jobs.

291
designer Mike Brower
illustrator Tracy Sabin
design firm Mires Design
client MG Swing Company
Logo for a painting contractor specializing in faux.

292
designer Deborah Hom
art director Scott Mires
illustrator Tracy Sabin
design firm Mires Design
client Harcourt Brace & Co.
Logo for a T-shirt commemorating completion of a series of educational text books for children.

288

289

290

291

292

293
designer   Russell Leong
design firm   Russell Leong Design
client   City of Palo Alto Parks &
Recreation
Logo for Palo Alto's annual black
and white ball.

294
designer   Dickson A. Keyser
design firm   Cotsifas/Keyser Design Services
client   JDM Catering Co.
Logo for a catering company with
an eclectic style.

295
designer   Russell Leong
design firm   Russell Leong Design
client   Richardson Architects
Logo for an architectural firm.

296
designer   Becca Smidt
art director   Sam Smidt
design firm   Sam Smidt Inc.
client   Versaggi Bio-Communications
Logo for a bio-medical
marketing/communications firm.

297
designer   Nita Ybarra
art director   Jeffrey Shurtz
design firm   Shurtz/Capriotti
client   Sun Microsystems
Logo for Sun Ware catalog.

293

294

295

296   VERSAGGI BIO COMMUNICATIONS

297

298
designer Calvin Chiu
design firm Edcal Design
client Herbert von Karajan Club
Logo for a classical music
conductors club.

299
designer Martha Newton Furman
design firm Martha Newton Furman Design &
Illustration
client San José Chamber Orchestra
Logo for a professional chamber
orchestra.

299A
designer Martha Newton Furman
design firm Martha Newton Furman Design &
Illustration
client San José State University School
of Music & Dance
Logo for Center for Research in
Electro-Acoustic Music.

300
designer Paul Morales
art director Robert Kastigar
illustrator Georgia Deaver
design firm Halleck Design Group
client San Jose Symphony
Logo for the symphony orchestra

301
designer Joe Miller
design firm Joe Miller's Company
client KSJS Public Radio
Logo for an eclectic music and
public affairs radio station.

297

298

299

SAN JOSE SYMPHONY

300

301

302
designer   Rod Dyer
design firm   Dyer/Mutchnick Group Inc.
client   Universal Records
Logo for a record company.

303
designer   Laurie Carrigan
art director   Steve Turner
design firm   Hausman Design
client   IBSS Business Group
Logo for a semi-conductor
manufacturer.

304
designer   Bill Corridori
art director   Keith Bright
design firm   Bright Strategic Design
client   KCET Store of Knowledge
Logo for a retail store selling books,
CD ROMs, etc. on knowledge,
education and creativity
worldwide.

305
designers   José A. Serrano
Miguel Perez
illustrator   Tracy Sabin
design firm   Mires Design
client   Found Stuff Paper Works
Logo for recycled organically
grown cotton.

306
designer   Steven Morris
design firm   Steven Morris Design
client   Arts al Fresco
Logo for arts, music and
dance festivals.

307
designer   Lewis Harrison
illustrator   Patrice Roberts
design firm   Lewis Harrison Design, Inc.
client   Cibacs
Logo for an educational program
for international and
communication studies.

302

303

304

305

306

307

308
designer   Mary Anne Mastandrea
art director   Elizabeth Keenan
design firm   Mastandrea Design
client   Heavenly Ski Resort
           Logo for the ski resort's 40th
           anniversary.

309
designer   José A. Serrano
illustrator   Tracy Sabin
design firm   Mires Design
client   Deleo Clay Tile Company
           Logo for a new line of clay tiles to
           be sold in Hawaii.

310
designer   Julia Becker Foug
art director   Lisa Capriotti
design firm   Shurtz/Capriotti
client   Beaver Creek Lodge
           Logo for a bistro/restaurant in
           Colorado, USA.

311
designer   Paul Weingartner
design firm   pw Design
client   California Primary Care Association
           Logo for a non-profit medical
           association.

312
designer   Mike Cotsifas
design firm   Cotsifas/Keyser Design Services
client   Boulders Golf Center
           Logo for a golf driving range.

313
designer   Daren L. Passolt
design firm   Visualizer Design Studios
client   Molokai Magic
           Logo for maker of custom stained
           glass art and windows.

314
designer   Daren L. Passolt
design firm   Visualizer Design Studios
client   Mystic Mountain
           Logo created for an all natural
           hand made soap company.

315
designer   Barbara Brown
design firm   Barbara Brown Marketing and
           Design
client   Channel Islands Properties
           Logo for Channel Islands Properties
           reflecting a local natural landmark.

308

309

310

311

312

313

314

315

316
designer   Diane Kuntz
dillustrator   Linda Eberle
design firm   Diane Kuntz Design
client   UniHealth
               Logo for a corporate health care
               management program.

317
designers   Dorothy Remington
               Joanna Wiraatmadja
art director   Doug Akagi
design firm   Akagi Remington
client   Hacienda Corazon
               Logo for a high-end residential
               community in the Philippines.

318
designer   Jeff Kahn
design firm   Kahn Design
client   Honey Rose Baking Co.
               Logo for a health food bakery.

319
designers   Larry Vigon
               Brian Jackson
design firm   Vigon/Ellis
client   Elixir
               Logo for a Chinese herbal
               remedy store.

320
designer   Ray Wood
art director   Keith Bright
design firm   Bright Strategic Design
client   California Community Foundation
               Logo for a foundation to raise and
               distribute funds to worthy causes
               and institutions.

321
designer   Ray Wood
art director   Keith Bright
design firm   Bright Strategic Design
client   The State of California
               Environmental Protection Agency
               Logo for agency protecting the
               environment.

322
designer   Daren L. Passolt
design firm   Visualizer Design Studios
client   Cloverleaf Pre Schools
               Logo created for Cloverleaf
               Private Pre Schools.

316

317

318

elixir

Tonics & Teas

319

CALIFORNIA
COMMUNITY
FOUNDATION

320

Cal / EPA

321

Cloverleaf Pre Schools

322

323
designer Jeff Ivarson
design firm Ivarson Design Group
client Fenwick Willow
Logo for a manufacturer of high
quality fishing rods.

324
designer Ramsey Said
art director Jeff Ivarson
illustrator Chet Phillips
design firm Ivarson Design Group
client 3M Pharmaceutical
Logo for Zartra
pharmaceutical creme.

325
designer Jill Thayer
design firm Jill Thayer Associates
client Rio Bravo Resort
Logo for a resort located in the
Southern Sierras.

326
designer Qris Yamashita
art director Rod Dyer
design firm Dyer/Mutchnick Group Inc.
client Evergreen Entertainment
Logo for a Hallmark Film
Production Company.

327
designer Joe Miller
design firm Joe Miller's Company
client Shade
Logo for an etherial rock group.

328
designer Glenn Johnson
art director Jerry Takigawa
design firm Jerry Takigawa Design
client Natural Selection Foods
Logo for growers and
marketers of specialty
salads and organic
vegetables.

329
designer Paul Weingartner
design firm pw Design
client Settimana Fiorentina
Logo for a festival
of Italian culture.

WILLOW

323

324

An Extraordinary Resort

325

326

327

NATURAL SELECTION FOODS

328

SETTIMANA FIORENTINA

329

330
designer   Ron Miriello
illustrator   Michelle Aranda
design firm   Miriello Grafico, Inc.
client   Tomato's
              Logo for an Italian restaurant.

331
designer   Qris Yamashita
art director Rod Dyer
design firm   Dyer/Mutchnick Group Inc.
client   Cafe America
              Logo for a restaurant.

332
designer   John Ball
illustrator   Nadeem Zzidi
design firm   Mires Design
client   Woodstock Idea Factory
              Logo for a creative consultant.

333
designer   Joe Miller
art director Mai Nguyen, Quantum
design firm   Joe Miller's Company
client   Fireball
              Logo for a disk drive manufacturer.

334
designer   Linda Kahn
art director Micki Wilson
design firm   Frank Templeton Inc.
client   Micki Wilson/Franklin
              Templeton Inc.
              Logo for a new software program
              to access clients' accounts.

335
designer   Debbie Smith
art director Leila Daubert
design firm   Addis Group
client   Compton's Home Library
              Logo for a software business.

330

331

332

333

334

335

336

336
designer   Barbara Bettis
art director   John Hamagami
design firm   Hamagami/Carroll & Associates
client   Disneyland Grad Nite 1995
          Logo for graduating high school
          seniors program.

337
designer   Mary Anne Mastandrea
art director   Elizabeth Keenan
design firm   Studio 77/Goldberg Moser O'Neill
client   Number Nine
          Logo for a high-tech company..

338
designer   Barbara Bettis
art director   John Hamagami
design firm   Hamagami/Carroll & Associates
client   Disneyland Grad Nite 1994
          Logo for graduating high school
          seniors program.

339
designer   Paula Sugarman
illustrator   Brad Maur
design firm   Page Design, Inc.
client   KVIE
          Logo for Channel 6 public
          television station.

337

338

339

340
designers   Doyle Harrison
            Mary Evelyn McGough
art director Mike Salisbury
design firm Mike Salisbury
            Communications, Inc.
client   Gamers
            Logo for online internet gaming.

341
designer   Mary Evelyn McGough
art director Mike Salisbury
design firm Mike Salisbury
            Communications, Inc.
client   Rage
            Logo for a magazine.

342
designer   Margo Chase
design firm Margo Chase Design
client   Westland Graphics
            "May" logo for a promotional
            calendar.

343
designer   Kenneth Lewis
design firm Kenneth Lewis Design
client   Leo Gong Photography
            Logo for a photography studio.

344
art director Patti Judd
design firm Juddesign
client   Seating Concepts
            Logo for an international theater
            seating manufacturer.

345
designer   Jon Lagda
art director Ron Scheibel
design firm Hunt, Rook & Scheibel
client   Moss Micro
            Logo for a software
            engineering company.

346
designer   Barbara Bettis
art director Justin Carroll
design firm Hamagami/Carroll & Associates
client   20th Century Fox
            Logo for "The X Files"
            television program.

340

341

342

343

344

MOSS MICRO™

345

346

347
designer   Russell Leong
design firm   Russell Leong Design
client   E3
               Logo for a manufacturer of digital
               sampling keyboards.

348
designer   Amy Williams
art director   Patti Judd
design firm   Juddesign
client   The Dakota Group
               Logo for a film and video
               production company.

349
designer   Mary Anne Mastandrea
design firm   Mastandrea Design
client   Mastandrea Design
               Logo for the design firm.

350
designer   Rod Dyer
design firm   Dyer/Mutchnick Group Inc.
client   Leo Burnett/Sony
               Retail logo for Sony
               Maximum Television.

351
designer   Martha Newton Furman
design firm   Martha Newton Furman Design &
               Illustration
client   Theresa Vargo Photography
               Logo for photographer
               Theresa Vargo.

352
designer   Russell Leong
illustrator   Meredith Chew
design firm   Russell Leong Design
client   Exponential
               Logo for a manufacturer of
               computer chips.

347

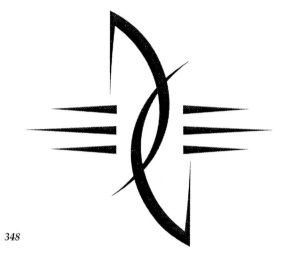

348

349

SURROUND SOUND™

350

351

exponential

352

353

354

353
designer   Peter Sargent
art director   Peter Sargent
design firm   Sargent & Berman
client   Advanced Travel Management
              Logo for a travel agency.

354
designer   Glenn Sakamoto
art director   Rod Dyer
design firm   Dyer/Mutchnick Group Inc.
client   Players Network
              Logo for a Las Vegas
              television network.

355
designer   Qris Yamashita
art director   Rod Dyer
design firm   Dyer/Mutchnick Group Inc.
client   O'Melveny & Myers LLP
              Logo for a law firm.

356
designer   Peter Cook
design firm   Dyer/Mutchnick Group Inc.
client   Gramercy Pictures
              Logo for a motion picture company.

357
designer   Rod Dyer
design firm   Dyer/Mutchnick Group Inc.
client   Bregman/Baer Productions, Inc.
              Logo for a motion picture
              production company.

355

356

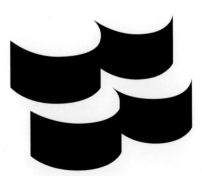

357

358
designer   Jamie Graupner
art director John White
design firm   White Design, Inc.
client   Barrington Consulting Group
              Logo for legal consultants for
              business and engineering.

359
designer   Glenn Sakamoto
art director Rod Dyer
design firm   Dyer/Mutchnick Group Inc.
client   Ironhawk Design Co.
              Logo for an ironwork artisan.

360
designer   Greg Lindy
design firm   Rey International
client   AMP
              Logo for a magazine-like website
              for MCA records.

361
designer   Gregory Thomas
design firm   Gregory Thomas Associates
client   Walden Partners
              Logo for a designer and
              manufacturer of pop displays for
              Fortune 500 companies.

362
designer   Hun Wynn
art director Rod Dyer
design firm   Dyer/Mutchnick Group Inc.
client   Abrams Artists Agency
              Logo for a creative talent agency.

363
designers   Jennifer Morla
             Craig Bailey
design firm   Morla Design
client   San Francisco Production Group
              Logo for a video production facility
              specializing in animation, sound
              and film.

358

359

360

WALDEN PARTNERS

361

ABRAMS ARTISTS AGENCY

362

363

364
designer   Daren L. Passolt
design firm Visualizer Design Studios
client   Tactic
Logo for a database software
company.

365
designer   Daren L. Passolt
design firm Visualizer Design Studios
client   Integrated Facilities Resources
Corporate identity created for an
internally operated facilities
solution provider.

366
designer   Daren L. Passolt
design firm Visualizer Design Studios
client   Apple Computer, Inc.
Created for a product support
booklet for Latin American and the
Caribbean marketplace.

367
designer   Brad Maur
art director Paul Page
design firm Page Design, Inc.
client   Reebok
Logo for a Reebok-sponsored
expedition to climb the Mt K2 on
the North Ridge.

368
designer   Daren L. Passolt
design firm Visualizer Design Studios
client   Rhetorex
Tapi Express logo created for a
voice activated software package.

369
designers   Larry Vigon
            Marc Yeh
illustrator   Marc Yeh
design firm Vigon/Ellis
client   Matinee Entertainment
Logo for an animation production
company.

364

365

366

367

368

matinee
ENTERTAINMENT

369

370   LOS ANGELES

371

A C I ™

WORLDWIDE DISTRIBUTION

372

370
designer   Taleen Bedikian
art director Ray Wood
design firm Bright Strategic Design
client   Los Angeles Convention &
           Visitors Bureau
           Logo designed to bring visitors and
           conventions to Los Angeles.

371
designer   William Kent
art director Tricia Rauen
design firm Buz Design Group
client   Adelson Entertainment
           Logo for entertainment
           productions.

372
designers   Jann Bielenberg
           Lea Horrmitz
design firm Bielenberg Design Group
client   ACI
           Logo for a film distribution
           company.

373
designer   Darlene McElroy
design firm Darlene McElroy Design
client   Darlene McElroy Design
           Logo for a design studio.

374
designer   Darlene McElroy
design firm Darlene McElroy Design
client   Maria Piscopo
           Logo for an artists and
           photographers representative and
           art consultant.

375
designer   Gina Simpson
design firm Sexton/Simpson Design
client   Miller Construction
           Logo for a construction company.

373

DARLENE M CELROY

DESIGN

Illustration

374

MARIA PISCOPO

DAN MILLER
CONSTRUCTION

375

376
designer   Ray Wood
art director   Keith Bright
design firm   Bright Strategic Design
client   Mercury Wave Craft
               Logo for manufacturers of a
               new jet ski.

377
designer   Ray Wood
art director   Keith Bright
design firm   Bright Strategic Design
client   Bullwhackers
               Logo for a casino and
               entertainment center.

378
designer   Mamoru Shimokochi
art director   Anne Reeves
design firm   Shimokochi/Reeves
client   Kagoshima
               Proposed logo for the
               prefecture of Japan.

379
designer   Mark Allen
art director   Cynthia Kinney
design firm   Mark Allen Design
client   Justice Records
               Logo for a tribute CD for
               Willie Nelson.

380
designers   Dorothy Remington
               Amelie Von Fluegge
illustrator   Amelie Von Fluegge
design firm   Akagi Remington
client   Remington Design
               Logo for a graphic design studio.
               Initials stand for Dorothy
               Remington and Remington Design.

381
designer   Jeff Heesch
art director   Michael Stinson
design firm   Stinson Design
client   Jennifer and Jeffrey Heesch
               Logo for the Heesch's wedding.

376

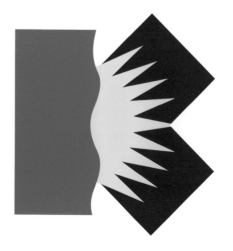

377

378

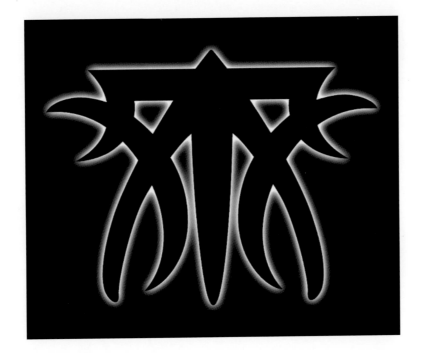

379

380

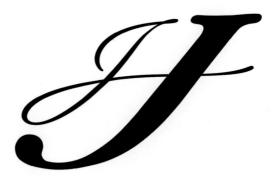

381

382
designer | Mark Kawakami
design firm | M-Studios
client | Honda
Logo for an automotive manufacturer.

383
designers | Larry Vigon
| Brian Jackson
design firm | Vigon/Ellis
client | Julie Dennis
Logo for a photographer.

384
designers | Kathryn Thornton
| Laura Mische
art director | Linda Warren
design firm | Warren Group
client | Creative Wonder
Logo for an event production company.

385
designer | Barbara D. Cummings
design firm | B.D. Cummings/Illustration
client | DAA
Logo for a full-service advertising agency.

386
designer | Gordon Mortensen
illustrator | John Bleck
design firm | Mortensen Design
client | Rendition
Logo for high-speed texture wrapping and 3-D rendering for animation on PCs.

387
designer | Dickson A. Keyser
design firm | Design Services of Dickson A. Keyser
client | Weaver Surfboards
Logo for a surfboard shaper.

388
designer | Jeffry Burne
design firm | Burne Design
client | Paramount Fasteners
Logo for a distributor of bolts, nuts, screws and other fasteners.

382

383 JULIE DENNIS

384 Creative Wonder

385

rendition

386

387

PARAMOUNT FASTENERS

388

147

389
designer — Paul Morales
design firm — Onyx Design Inc.
client — Double Hull Tankers Ltd.
Logo for a double hull tanker
consultant.

390
designer — Mark Kawakami
design firm — M-Studios
client — Cru Clothing
Logo for a sports apparel company

391
designer — Howie Idelson
design firm — Urban Image Studio
client — Pacific Athletic Club

392
designers — Larry Vigon
Brian Jackson
design firm — Vigon/Ellis
client — If..
Logo for high tech database
products.

393
designers — Larry Vigon
Brian Jackson
design firm — Vigon/Ellis
client — Vigon/Ellis
Logo for a brand development and
graphic design group.

394
designer — Kim Sage
art director — Petrula Vrontikis
design firm — Vrontikis Design Office
client — Playpen
Logo for film and television
motion graphics.

395
designer — Paula Sugarman
design firm — Page Design, Inc.
client — Zellerbach Paper
Logo for a paper merchant's paper
specification service for the
design industry.

389

390

391

392

393

394

CLUB

395

396
designer   Becca Smidt
design firm Becca Smidt
client   Googie Tours
             Logo for a company giving tours of
             historical 1950s coffee shops,
             diners and bowling alleys in L.A.

397
designer   Becca Smidt
art director Sam Smidt
design firm Sam Smidt Inc.
client   Turner Martin
             Logo for a gift store selling hand
             made objects for the home.

398
designer   Jann Bielenberg
illustrator Eric David
design firm Bielenberg Design Group
client   The Cassie Awards
             Logo for telecast awards show for
             excellence in the casino/
             resort entertainment industry.

399
designer   Mark Allen
art director Jon Sparrman
design firm Mark Allen Design
client   Warner Bros.
             Logo for a proposed movie title.

400
designer   Howie Idelson
design firm Urban Image Studio
client   Style Kings Clothing

401
designer   Mark Allen
art director Bernie Urban
design firm Mark Allen Design
client   Marketing Foundations/
             Superior Coffee and Foods
             Logo for a coffee brand.

396

397

398

399

U.S.A. Quality

400

Signatures

401

402
designer Howie Idelson
design firm Urban Image Studio
client Pacific Athletic Club

403
designer Howie Idelson
design firm Urban Image Studio
client Zen Bakery

404
designer Howie Idelson
design firm Urban Image Studio
client Western Jeans

405
designer Howie Idelson
design firm Urban Image Studio
client Pro Circuit

406
designer Howie Idelson
design firm Urban Image Studio
client Gearbox/Renspeed
Logo for motorsport accessories

407
designer Howie Idelson
design firm Urban Image Studio
client Western Jeans

408
designer Howie Idelson
design firm Urban Image Studio
client Malibu Boardriders Club

402

403

404

405

RENSPEED

406

407

408

409
designers   Mark Allen
               Harrison Allen
art director   Gail Harrison
design firm   Mark Allen Design
client   Hanna-Barbera
               Logo for the 60th anniversary of
               "The Wizard of Oz."

410
designer   Mark Allen
art director   Matti Leshem
design firm   Mark Allen Design
client   S.C. Headline News
               Web site logo for
               "The Second City."

411
designer   Mark Allen
art director   Laurel Buerk
design firm   Mark Allen Design
client   Outdoor Recreation Group/Oblique
               Logo for Snowboard merchandise.

412
designer   Mark Allen
art directors Stacie Seifrit
               Ann Wilkins
design firm   Mark Allen Design
client   KROQ
               Logo for a radio station talk show.

413
designer   Lisa Capriotti
design firm   Shurtz/Capriotti
client   Wells Fargo
               Logo for in-house use for approval
               on in-branch materials.

414
designer   Lisa Capriotti
illustrator   Dave Danz
design firm   Shurtz/Capriotti
client   Wells Fargo Bank
               Logo for an employee
               communications newsletter.

409

410

411

412

413

STAGELINES
WELLS FARGO

414

415
designer	Mark Allen
art director	Bill Leissring
design firm	Mark Allen Design
client	Miller Beer

Logo for an advertising campaign.

416
designer	Han Vu
art director	Jeffrey Shurtz
design firm	Shurtz/Capriotti
client	Hirsch Enterprises

Logo for a trade show event with a Mexican theme.

417
designer	John Ball
illustrator	Tracy Sabin
design firm	Mires Design
client	California Center For The Arts

Logo for an event at the arts center.

418
designer	Michael Cotsifas
art director	Marc Eis
design firm	Shugart Matson Marketing Communications
client	VISX

Logo for a manufacturer of lasers for vision correction.

419
designer	Dickson A. Keyser
design firm	Design Services of Dickson A. Keyser
client	Trash

Logo for a company making gifts from recycled products.

420
designer	Mark Allen
art director	Dave Parmley
design firm	Mark Allen Design
client	I-Storm

Logo for a website design company.

415

416

417

418

419

420

421
designers John Ball
Gale Spitzley
design firm Mires Design
client California Center For The Arts
Logo for an exhibition of animal-inspired artworks.

422
designers Deborah Hom
Scott Mires
illustrator Tracy Sabin
design firm Mires Design
client Ear To Ear
Logo for a music production/composing house.

423
designer Miguel Perez
art director John Ball
design firm Mires Design
client California Center For The Arts
Logo for a multi-disciplinary regional arts center.

424
designer Mike Brower
art director Scott Mires
illustrator Tracy Sabin
design firm Mires Design
client Food Group
Logo for a point of purchase poster to promote a new blended shake for Boyd's Coffee.

425
designer Miguel Perez
art director José A. Serrano
design firm Mires Design
client Donnelley Enterprise Solutions
Logo for a company that provides integrated information management services.

421

422

423

424

DONNELLEY
ENTERPRISE
SOLUTIONS
INCORPORATED

425

426
designer Mark Kawakami
design firm M-Studios
client Airtight
Logo for a wetsuit manufacturer.

427
designer Tracy E. Moon
design firm Aerial
client PC.IABP
Logo for personal computer/
medical equipment interface
software.

428
designer Mark Allen
design firm Mark Allen Design
client Chris Reade Communications
Logo for rep. who represents New
York rap groups.

429
designer José A. Serrano
illustrator Tracy Sabin
design firm Mires Design
client Chingones
Logo for custom street wear.

430
designer José A. Serrano
illustrator Tracy Sabin
design firm Mires Design
client Magic Carpet Books
Logo for a classic fantasy literature
book series.

431
designer José A. Serrano
illustrator Carl Vanderschuit
design firm Mires Design
client Agassi Enterprises
Logo for a new gripping powder.

426

427

428

429

MAGIC
CARPET
BOOKS

430

FUSION

431

432
designer   Tracy E. Moon
design firm Aerial
client   Impact Unlimited
            Logo for exhibit and event design
            and marketing services.

433
designer   Tracy E. Moon
design firm Aerial
client   Lenox Roomn
            Logo for an upscale, upper east
            side Manhattan restaurant.

434
designer   Tracy E. Moon
design firm Aerial
client   Datascope
            Logo for a leader in innovative
            tools, technology and equipment
            for the healthcare industry.

435
designer   Tracy E. Moon
design firm Aerial
client   Idiom
            Logo for a strategic naming firm.

436
designer   Tracy E. Moon
design firm Aerial
client   Beach House
            Logo for a seaside hotel/
            condominium development.

437
designer   Tracy E. Moon
design firm Aerial
client   Phoenix Network
            Logo for telecommunications
            billing services.

432

LENOX
R R O O O M

433

Datascope

434

id´i·om

435

Beach House

436

PhoenixNetwork.

437

438
designer Tracy E. Moon
design firm Aerial
client ACA JOE
Logo for men's casual clothing.

439
designer Tracy E. Moon
illustrator John Mattos
design firm Aerial
client Hotel Bohéme
Logo for a hotel/hospitality industry.

440
designer Steven Morris
design firm Steven Morris Design
client RPM Color
Logo for a color scanning, film
output service bureau.

441
designer Miguel Perez
art director John Ball
design firm Mires Design
client Copeland Reis Talent Agency
Logo for a talent agency.

442
designer Pilar Dowell
art director Pilar Dowell
design firm Dowell Design
client Intenational Hapkido Karate
Association
Logo for a Karate Association.

443
designer Tracy E. Moon
design firm Aerial
client Calypso Imaging
Logo for a digital color lab.

438

439

440

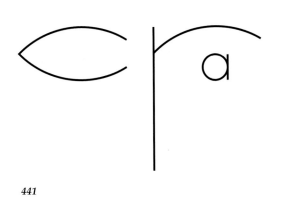

441

442

443

444
designer   Maria Wang-Horn
design firm   Wang/Hutner
client   Auctionet
Logo for a computer hardware
auction company on the internet.

445
designer   Thomas Harley Bond
design firm   SBG Partners
client   Hewlett Packard
Logo for products within
Hewlett Packard's Interactive
Entertainment Division.

446
designer   John Hopkins
design firm   Hop Art
client   Hop Art
Logo representing designer's own
graphic design studio.

447
designers   Brian Jacobson
    Jeanne Namkung
art director   Thomas McNulty
illustrator   Jeanne Namkung
design firm   Profile Design
client   Mariani Nut Company
Logo for a grower and
processor of raw nuts in
California's Central Valley.

448
designer   Lena Tonseth
art director   Kenichi Nishiwaki
design firm   Profile Design
client   San Francisco Opera Guild
Logo for the guild which supports
and promotes education of the arts
and raises funds for the San
Francisco Opera.

449
designer   Brian Jacobson
art director   Thomas McNulty
illustrator   Liz Wheaton
design firm   Profile Design
client   Dr. McDougall's Right Foods
Logo for a developer and
manufacturer of healthy foods.

444

445

446

447

448

449

450
designer   Howard Ian Schiller
design firm   TL-R & Associates
client   Insite
           Logo for a website marketing and
           development company.

451
designer   Riki Komachi
design firm   Riki Komachi
client   Venice 5/10 K
           Logo for the Venice 5/10 K run.

452
designer   John Sabel
art director   Rod Dyer
design firm   Dyer/Mutchnick Group Inc.
client   Sensa
           Logo for fresh, new herbal drinks
           with natural flavors.

453
designer   Qris Yamashita
art director   Rod Dyer
design firm   Dyer/Mutchnick Group Inc.
client   Big Ticket Television
           Logo for comedy programming.

454
designers   Jeanne Namkung
           Anthony Luk
art directors   Kenichi Nishiwaki
           Russell Baker
design firm   Profile Design
client   Project Open Hand
           Logo for a non-profit
           organization in San
           Francisco which provides
           meals, groceries and
           health servies to
           people with AIDS.

455
designer   Peter Nam
design firm   Peter Nam Design
client   San Francisco Tea
           Symposium
           Logo for educational
           seminars on tea.

450

451

452

453

454

455

456

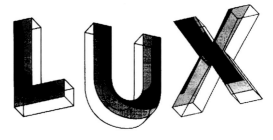

457

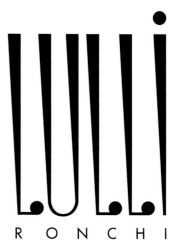

458

459

460

461

462

463
designer | Mark Jones
art directors | Primo Angeli
| Carlo Pagoda
art director | Primo Angeli
client | Wilbur-Ellis Company
Logo for a company specializing in agricultural products for the international market.

464
designers | Jenny Baker
| Mark Jones
art directors | Primo Angeli
| Ron Hoffman
illustrator | Liz Wheaton
design firm | Primo Angeli Inc.
client | Ferris & Roberts
Logo for an herbal line of imported English teas with a perceived established English heritage.

465
designers | Terrence Tong
| Ed Cristman
art directors | Primo Angeli
| Carlo Pagoda
illustrator | Robert Evans
design firm | Primo Angeli Inc.
client | Mariani Packing Company
Logo for a line of dried fruit that reinforces the fresh fruit origins.

466
designer | Bill Corridori
art director | Keith Bright
design firm | Bright Strategic Design
client | Gratis Restaurant
Logo for a gourmet restaurant serving fat-free cuisine.

467
designer | Maria Wang-Horn
design firm | Wang/Hutner Design
client | 1st Byte
Logo for a computer hardware auction company on the internet.

468
designer | Maria Wang-Horn
design firm | Wang/Hutner Design
client | Vertigo
Logo for a restaurant and bar.

463

464

465

GRAT!S

466

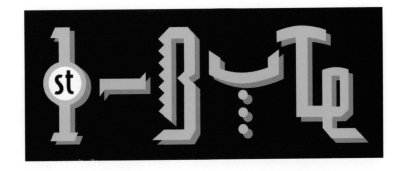

467

RESTAURANT & BAR

468

BIRTHMARK PRODUCTIONS

469

470

ACQUARELLO
THE TRAVEL ARTIST

471

469
designer   Jeni Olsen
design firm JO Design
client   Green T.V.
Logo for a cable television show which profiles environmentally aware companies and people.

470
designer   Jeni Olsen
design firm JO Design
client   The Grapeline
Logo for a comany offering computer network installations and software support for retail systems in wineries.

471
designer   Steve Twigger
art director Rod Dyer
design firm Dyer/Mutchnick Group Inc.
client   Acquarello
Logo for a travel agent in Italy.

472
designers   Larry Vigon
           Brian Jackson
design firm Vigon/Ellis
client   Mr. Lucky's
Logo for a restaurant.

473
designer   Glenn Sakamoto
art director Rod Dyer
design firm Dyer/Mutchnick Group Inc.
client   Tixa Technology
Logo for a software/hardware company.

472

TIXA TECHNOLOGY

473

474
designer | Sam Lising
art director | Petrula Vrontikis
design firm | Vrontikis Design Office
client | Greenhood & Company
Logo for new media
technology experts.

475
designers | Chip Toll
 | Judy Radiche
art director | Primo Angeli
design firm | Primo Angeli Inc.
client | Spectrum Foods
Logo for the Tutto Mare restaurant.

476
designer | Russell Leong
design firm | Russell Leong Design
client | Betelnut
Logo for a Pan-Asian restaurant.

477
designer | Rod Dyer
design firm | Dyer/Mutchnick Group Inc.
client | Monk Recording Group
Logo for a cutting edge recording
company.

478
designer | Chris Cava
art director | Rod Dyer
design firm | Dyer/Mutchnick Group Inc.
client | Fremont Street Experience
Logo for Fremont Street
Experience, Las Vegas.

474

475

476

477

478

479
designer	Daren L. Passolt
design firm	Visualizer Design Studios
client	Amdahl Corporation
	Logo Created for the
	25th anniversary of Amdahl.

480
designer	Aaron Atchison
art director	Tricia Rauen
design firm	Buz Design Group
client	The Loop
	Logo for an internet server.

481
designer	Tracy Titus
art director	Paul Page
illustrator	Kimberly Bickel
design firm	Page Design, Inc.
client	TheraCare Rehab
	Logo for a provider of care for
	elderly people through
	rehabilitation.

482
designer	Darlene McElroy
design firm	Darlene McElroy Design
client	Timbuktu
	Logo for a folk and tribal shop.

483
designer	Kelli Kunkle-Day
art director	Tricia Rauen
design firm	Buz Design Group
client	Rock Architects
	Logo for an architectural firm.

484
designer	Ron Miriello
design firm	Miriello Grafico, Inc.
client	Lux Kahvé
	Logo for a restaurant/lounge.

479

480

481

482

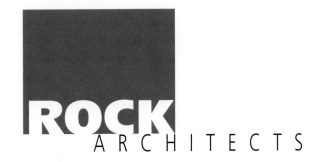

483

484

485
designers   Larry Vigon
               Marc Yeh
design firm   Vigon/Ellis
client   LAX
               Logo for the Los Angeles
               Department of Airports
               renovation project.

486
designers   Larry Vigon
               Marc Yeh
art director Todo Reublin
illustrator Michael Elins
design firm   Vigon/Ellis
client   DreamWorks SKG
               Logo for the music division of
               DreamWorks.

487
designer   Kimberly Bickel
design firm   Page Design, Inc.
client   Amongst Friends
               Logo for a photographer who
               concentrates on black-and-white
               portraits and then hand tints them.

488
designer   Daren L. Passolt
design firm   Visualizer Design Studios
client   Rhetorex
               RealCT logo created for a voice
               activated software program.

489
designer   Cheryl Pelly
design firm   Pelly Design Associates
client   Lock Shock
               Logo for mountain bike shock
               absorbers.

490
designer   Cheryl Pelly
design firm   Designworks/USA
client   Deere
               Proposed logo for the John Deere
               industrial tractor division.

485

486

487

488

489

490

491
designers   Philippe Becker
               Rolando Rosler
art director   Primo Angeli
design firm   Primo Angeli Inc.
client   Omnihost
               Logo for worldwide
               communications software.

492
designer   Terrence Tong
art directors Primo Angeli
               Ron Hoffman
design firm   Primo Angeli Inc.
client   ATEC
               Logo for a sports equipment
               company that specializes in
               baseball training equipment.

493
designer   Brad Maur
design firm   Page Design, Inc.
client   Magnum Gear
               Logo for a manufacturer of outdoor
               and rugged footwear.

494
designers   Primo Angeli
               Ian McClean
art directors Rolando Rosler
               Mark Crumpacker
design firm   Primo Angeli Inc.
client   Lavazza
               Logo designed for the entry
               of an Italian coffee into the
               American market.

495
designer   Lissa Patrizi
design firm   Patrizi Designs
client   Jeff's Decorative Finishes
               Logo for custom painting and
               art furniture.

496
designers   Daren L. Passolt
               Paul Schatzel
design firm   Visualizer Design Studios
client   The MACgician
               Logo for a Macintosh networking
               solution service.

491

492

493

494

495

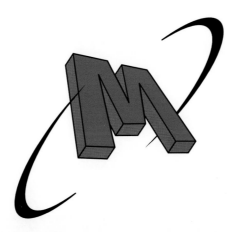

The MACgician

496

497

498

499

500

497
designer Sarah Tannas
design firm Tannas Design
client Cafe Romantico
Proposed logo for a small
Italian cafe.

498
designer Daren L. Passolt
design firm Visualizer Design Studios
client Advantage
Logo created for an online laptop
that provides on-demand
information to the sales force and
field members.

499
designer Daren L. Passolt
design firm Visualizer Design Studios
client Amdahl Corporation
Proposed revision to update the
look of their existing logo.

500
designer Sarah Tannas
design firm Tannas Design
client Amazonia
Logo for an upscale Brazilian
clothing company.

501
designer Daren L. Passolt
design firm Visualizer Design Studios
client Disaster Contingency Solutions
Logo created for a group that
helps companies get up and
running again after any type of
natural disaster.

502
designer Daren L. Passolt
design firm Visualizer Design Studios
client Amdahl Corporation
Created for purchasing department
suppliers guide booklet.

501

502

503
designer	John Smeaton
art director	Scott A. Mednick
design firm	Think New Ideas
client	Upper Deck Authenticated

Logo for a company specializing in authentic sport collectibles.

504
designer	John Smeaton
design firm	Smeaton Design
client	MSA

Logo for architect Mark Smeaton.

505
designer	Daren L. Passolt
design firm	Visualizer Design Studios
client	Repro Graphics

Created for an internal reproduction graphics department.

506
designer	Cheryl Pelly
design firm	Pelly Design Associates for Terry Ruscin Advertising, Inc.
client	Rancho Bernardo Health Center

Logo for a retirement/health care facility.

507
designer	Cheryl Pelly
design firm	C.W.A., Inc.
client	Humetrix

Logo for a manufacturer of instruments that measure human heart rates, blood pressure, etc.

503

504

505

RANCHO BERNARDO

HEALTH CENTER

506

507

508
designers Mary Evelyn McGough
Mike Hand
art director Mike Salisbury
design firm Mike Salisbury
Communications, Inc.
client Fiction Now

509
designer Mary Evelyn McGough
art director Mike Salisbury
design firm Mike Salisbury
Communications, Inc.
client Mike Salisbury
Communications, Inc.
Logo for a graphic design and
advertising firm.

510
designer Barbara Bettis
design firm Hamagami/Carroll & Associates
client DirecTV
Logo for satellite TV programming
distributors.

511
designer Dickson Keyser
design firm Northern California Chapter of
SEGD
client Noe Valley Ministry
Logo for a multi-use community
center for a San Francisco
neighborhood.

512
designer Joe Miller
design firm Joe Miller's Company
client Works
Logo for a non-profit alternative art
and performance space.

513
designer Lewis Harrison
design firm Lewis Harrison Design, Inc.
client Cool Cottons
Logo for a children's casual
clothing line made only with 100%
cotton in mostly pastel colors.

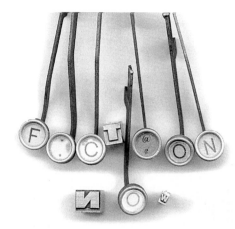

508

509

510

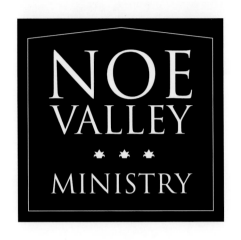

511

512

COOL COTTONS™

513

514
designer   Jeff Ishikawa
design firm   GDA Technology Advertising
client   GDA Technology Advertising
Logo for advertising agency
specializing in high-tech clients.

515
designer   Leslie Oki
art director   Paul Marciano
design firm   Guess? Inc.
client   Guess? Interactive
Logo for an apparel company.

516
designer   Dickson Keyser
art director   Nancy Daniels
design firm   The GNU Group
client   Lalka
Logo for a Sheraton
hotel/restaurant in
Warsaw, Poland.

517
designer   Archie Ong
art director   Sam Smidt
design firm   Inhaus Design
client   Neon
Logo for a non-profit organization's
online service.

518
designer   Larimie Garcia
design firm   gig
client   Larry A. Garcia Landscape
Company
Logo for a landscape installation
and maintenence company.

519
designer   Edoardo Chavarin
art director   Larimie Garcia
design firm   gig
client   Innovation Snowboards
Logo for a snowboard
manufacturer.

520
designer   Jon Lagda
art director   Ron Scheibel
design firm   Hunt, Rook & Scheibel
client   WildStuffs
Logo for a line of toasted
ravioli appetizers.

514

http://www.guess.com

515

516

517

518

519

Wild Stuffs™

520

521
designer Jon Lagda
design firm K3/Kato Kreative Koncepts
client Boomslang
Logo for an alternative rock band.

522
designer Brian Lorenz
design firm Lorenz Advertising & Design, Inc.
client New England Velodrome
Committee
Logo for a fund-raising
committee whose purpose is to
generate interest in the fabrication
of a Boston Velodrome.

523
designer Tosh Kodama
art director Justin Carroll
design firm Hamagami/Carroll & Associates
client 20th Century Fox
Logo for the "Millennium"
television series on the cyclical
nature of life.

524
designer Margo Chase
art director Samantha Hart
design firm Margo Chase Design
client Gramercy Pictures
Logo for a feature film.

525
designer Archie Ong
design firm Inhaus Design
client Agenda
Logo for a bar/restaurant/
lounge.

526
designer Veronica See
art director Ken Anderson
design firm Fattal & Collins
client Disney Interactive
Logo for Disney software, a
division of Disney Inc.

521

522

523

524

525

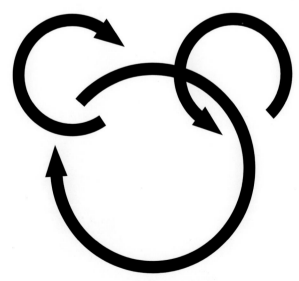

526

527
designer   Dianne O'Quinn Burke
design firm Burkarts
client   Logo for the San Luis Obispo
            Art Center.

528
designer   Larimie Garcia
art director Jeri Heiden
design firm gig
client   A&M Records
            Logo for recording artists.

529
designer   Larimie Garcia
art director Greg Gilmer
design firm gig
client   Warner Bros. Records
            Logo for a recording artist.

530
designer   Douglas Bogner
art directors David Kessler
             Jon Ianziti
design firm   Bullzye Design & Marketing
client   The Print Shop Deluxe Sampler
             Graphics
             Logo for an edutainment company
             specializing in CD ROM games and
             educational products.

531
designer   Douglas Bogner
art directors David Kessler
             Jon Ianziti
design firm   Bullzye Design & Marketing
client   Broderbund
             Logo for an edutainment company
             specializing in CD ROM games and
             educational products.

527

528

529

530

531

532
designer Minka Willig
design firm Minka Willig Design
client School of Visual and
Performing Arts
Logo for a photography, dance,
drama and graphic design school.

533
designer Mark Orton
art director John Hamagami
design firm Hamagami/Carroll & Associates
client Have A Ball
Logo for a calendar of all
scheduled NBA games.

534
designer Veronica See
art director Linda Posivak
design firm Fattal & Collins
client Castle Rock Entertainment
Logo for motion picture "Othello."

535
designer Jeni Olsen
art director Nancy Daniels
design firm The GNU Group
client Muju Resort
Logo for a year-round ski and
leisure resort in Korea.

536
designer J. Robert Faulkner
design firm J. Robert Faulkner Advertising
client UrbanXtreme
Logo for a line of specialized
backpacks.

532

533

534

MUJU

Land of Art and Nature

535

536

537

538

539

Handmade in California

DOLCE MIA

DOLCE MIA

Frames & Collectibles

540

541

542
designer   Archie Ong
design firm   Inhaus Design
client   Act Three
         Logo for a contemporary jazz club
         and lounge.

543
designer   Cheri Brewster
art director   Lois Brightwater
design firm   Brightwater Design Inc.
client   Specialty Brands Inc.
         Logo for a new product launch for
         Pacific Tortilla Kitchen.

544
designer   Sarah Tannas
art director   Ron Scheibel
design firm   Hunt, Rook & Scheibel
client   Santa Fe Cafe
         Proposed logo for a line of
         Southwestern entrees.

545
designer   Larimie Garcia
art director   Janet Levinson
design firm   gig
client   Warner Bros. Records
         Logo for "The Black Crowes"
         album cover, entitled "Three
         Snakes and a Charm."

542

543

544

545

Design Studios

Designers

Art Directors and Illustrators

Clients

Special Thanks

I would like to thank Lisa Woodard and Suzanne Rosentswieg for all the help and encouragement they gave me to keep Gerry's series going.

I would like to applaud Arpi Ermoyan for always being patient and understanding and for always getting the job done.

My hat is off to Harish Patel for doing a first class job of organizing and designing this book.

GREAT WORKS OF
INDIAN ART

Douglas Mannering

A Compilation of Works from the

BRIDGEMAN ART LIBRARY

Great Works of Indian Art

This edition first published in Great Britain in 1996 by
Parragon Book Service Limited
Units 13-17 Avonbridge Industrial Estate
Atlantic Road
Avonmouth
Bristol BS11 9QD

ISBN 0-7525-1141-6

Printed in Italy

Editors: Barbara Horn, Alexa Stace, Alison Stace, Tucker Slingsby Ltd
                      and Jennifer Warner

Designers: Robert Mathias • Pedro Prá-Lopez, Kingfisher Design Services

Typesetting/DTP: Frances Prá-Lopez, Kingfisher Design Services

Picture Research: Kathy Lockley

The publishers would like to thank Joanna Hartley at the Bridgeman Art Library
for her invaluable help.

Indian Art

'Indian art' is really shorthand for 'the art of the Indian sub-continent': that is modern India, Pakistan and Bangladesh. These political units are of course quite recent, and for most of history 'India' has satisfactorily described a geographical area, more often than not divided into many states.

The earliest Indian civilization is known only through archaeology. The Indus Valley culture, in the north-west, flourished between about 2500 and 1500 BC, and was evidently sophisticated and well organized. The small works of art that have been unearthed are fascinating, but their connection with any later period of Indian history is problematic.

At some point in the 2nd millennium BC, nomadic herders, known as the Aryans, descended through the passes of the north-west – always the main gateway into India for invaders – and occupied the northern plain from the Indus to the Ganges. The previous inhabitants were absorbed into Aryan society or driven down into the south of India.

For something like a thousand years, our only evidence about Aryan life lies in the *Vedas*, the earliest scriptures of Hinduism. Despite its long and complicated evolution, certain beliefs remained central to Hindu life – above all, the belief that the soul lives again and again, its lodging in each life depending on its past behaviour (*karma*). Equally durable was the caste system, which destined a person at birth to become a priest (*brahman*), warrior, freeman, artisan or slave.

Fuller historical records begin in the 6th century BC, when the first breakaways from Hinduism occurred. Both the Buddha and Mahavira (founder of Jainism) were historical figures whose lives have been recorded; in their different ways, both sought to show the individual a way out of the cycle of rebirth, suffering and death, discarding much of the myth and ritual associated with Hinduism.

Buddhism, which would become one of the great world religions, made great headway in India, especially during the period when the Maurya dynasty united most of the sub-continent. The greatest of the Mauryas, Ashoka (c 273-227 BC), proclaimed his adherence to Buddhism on tall lion-headed columns that are effectively the earliest surviving works of Indian art since the Indus Valley era.

The long history of Indian sculpture really begins in the early centuries AD, with centres at Gandhara, Mathura and Amaravati producing mainly Buddhist works; those at Gandhara in the north-west, where Persian and Greek influences had been felt for centuries, were in a 'un-Indian' style often labelled Greco-Buddhist. The sculpture of the Gupta period (AD 320-c 550) is generally held to represent one of the peaks of Indian art, although centuries of varied achievement were to follow.

In the 8th century, Arab armies occupied the Sind, and from about AD 1000 a series of Muslim invasions devastated much of India. Unlike earlier Indian religions, Islam was monotheistic and exclusive, destroying the temples and monasteries of its rivals. Buddhism, long past its zenith, virtually disappeared from India, but Hinduism, with a more directly emotional hold on the lives of the people, proved more resistant.

Painting already had a long history, but most major early works (notably the Buddhist paintings in the caves of Ajanta) have survived only in a seriously damaged condition. Then, in the late medieval period, miniature painting took on a new importance, especially once paper had replaced palm leaves. Miniature painting was by no means always small in format: the word comes from the Latin word for the medium once used, *minium* (red lead). The bold colours and stylized treatment of the Hindu miniature was submerged for a time by the Persian style introduced by the Mughals, Mongol-descended Muslim warriors who controlled much of India from about 1526. Modified by its new environment, the Mughal miniature brought a new and vivid realism to Indian art.

The decline of Mughal power in the 18th century led to the dispersal of the court artists and a final flowering of Hindu painting in the western and north-western (Punjab) states. The rise of a new imperial power, the British, hastened the decline of the Indian arts and, for better or worse, inaugurated a new phase in the history of the sub-continent.

◁ **Young Woman**
c 2300-1750 BC

Copper

THIS ELEGANT, ALOOF CREATURE
is often described as a dancing
girl, although in reality we know
nothing definite about her. Hers is
the only metal figure so far
recovered from the remains of
India's first civilization, centred on
the Indus Valley (modern
Pakistan) and flourishing between
about the mid-first and mid-
second millennium. The very
existence of the Indus Valley
civilization was unsuspected until
the mid-19th century, but
excavations in the 20th century
have shown that it supported large
cities such as Harrappa and
Mohenjo-Daro (where the figure
was found), although these are
modern labels, since the Indus
Valley script has never been
deciphered. Moreover, these sites
were models of town planning,
based on a grid system like that of
New York, with an astonishingly
capacious 'great bath'
(presumably for ritual purposes)
and a high citadel.

▷ **Head of a Camel**
c 2300-1750 BC

Terracotta

LIKE THE *YOUNG WOMAN* (opposite), this characterful head was found at Mohenjo-Daro, one of the chief centres of the Indus Valley civilization. The potter who shaped and fired it must have had considerable insight as well as technical skill, since he succeeded brilliantly in conveying the essential characteristics of the camel – its look of cud-chewing bad temper – while simplifying but not caricaturing the form of its head. All the works of art so far excavated from the Indus Valley sites are small (less than 20 cm/ 8 in high) and too limited in number to make serious judgements about: one copper figure, a few terracottas, and some figure carvings in steatite (soapstone, a very easily worked material). Much more numerous are little square seals made of steatite and engraved with brief pieces of script and splendidly observed buffaloes, elephants, rhinoceroses and other creatures; examples of these were found in Mesopotamia, indicating that the Indus Valley had trade contacts with the Near East in ancient times.

▷ **Head of a Foreigner**
3rd century BC

Sandstone

AT SOME POINT in the 2nd
millenium BC the Indus Valley
civilization collapsed. The causes
are unknown, and it is not even
clear whether the collapse was
sudden or gradual. During the
same long, obscure period, a new
people, the Aryans, came down
into India through the passes of
the north-west and occupied most
of the sub-continent. With them
they brought the Vedic religion
from which Hinduism developed;
but they seem to have had no art,
and to have positively distrusted
image-making. For a thousand
years or more the record is
virtually blank, until the
spectacular rise of the Maurya
dynasty led to the production of a
mainly Buddhist art. This carving
comes from Sarnath, a
particularly significant spot
because it was where the Buddha
preached his first sermon. The
polished appearance of the head is
characteristic of Maurya art,
produced by buffing the stone.

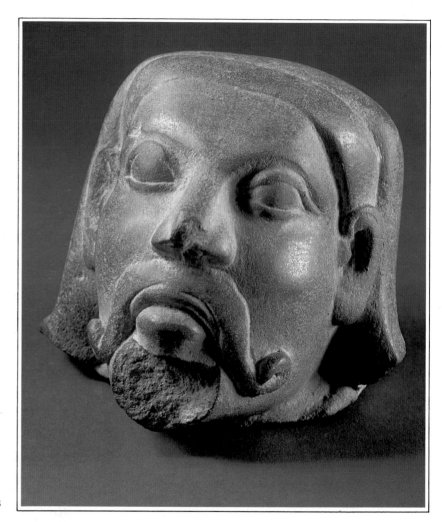

▷ **Yakshi** 2nd century BC

Terracotta

THE ARTISTIC REVIVAL that took place under the Maurya dynasty seems to have been a vigorous one, but relatively few works have survived from the period. The best-known objects are the pillars of carved and polished stone, raised by the Buddhist emperor Ashoka (c 273-232 BC); the relief carvings on Buddhist buildings (page 13); and a number of carvings of *yaksha* and *yakshi*. These were nature spirits, images of fertility and abundance whose origins were in local cults rather than the great religions. However, they were quickly incorporated into Buddhism and Hinduism; the *yakshi*, or female spirits, were often extremely voluptuous (page 16), and their appearance among the decorative devices on Buddhist buildings is liable to surprise a westerner, accustomed to a more rigid demarcation between spirit and flesh. The figure shown here is a rather unusual *yakshi* from Ahichchatra in northern India, elegantly dressed and taking up a stance that suggests an acquaintance with courts rather than hill and stream.

▷ The Buddha
c 3rd century AD

Schist

IN THE 6TH CENTURY BC, a new Indian creed was founded by Siddhartha Gautama. Born around 560 BC, Gautama belonged to the high-ranking warrior caste and grew up in comfortable circumstances. But, confronted with the facts of suffering and death, he embarked on an earnest quest for spiritual knowledge. Practising austerities brought him no nearer to the truth, but after meditating for 49 days under the Bodhi tree he experienced his awakening. Gautama became the Buddha ('Enlightened One') and spent the rest of his life preaching detachment from desire and a Middle Way between asceticism and indulgence. In the centuries following the Buddha's death (c486 BC) his teachings became widely popular, especially when they found a patron in the Mauryan emperor Ashoka, whose celebrated pillars record his remorse for the blood shed in his wars. For five centuries no image of the Buddha was permitted in Buddhist art, although symbols often indicated his presence. This grey schist head is in the Greco-Buddhist Gandhara style.

▷ Lintel from Sanchi
Early 1st century AD

Sandstone

ONE OF THE MOST IMPORTANT buildings in Indian Buddhist devotion is the *stupa*, which is essentially a monumental domed structure with a railing round it. It developed from the pre-Buddhist burial mound, and is still associated with death – or rather with the Buddha's release from the cycle of desire and suffering, for on his death he attained Nirvana. A *stupa* contained relics of the Enlightened One, and worshippers walked all round the interior as part of their devotions. The pillars, door and window frames and railings were lavishly decorated in low relief (that is, with the carved figures standing out only shallowly from the background). The Great Stupa at Sanchi is one of the most celebrated of early Buddhist *stupas*, built between the 3rd century BC and the 1st century AD. This lintel carries a carved figure of a fantastic animal, the griffin, sitting on a scroll. On the other side of the scroll is a surface carved in relief, with stylized plants, a woman, and a finely observed elephant.

Detail

▷ **Maitreya** 2nd century AD

Schist

DURING HIS LIFETIME, the Buddha expounded a philosophy rather than a set of religious doctrines, and presented himself as a purely human teacher. Later, legends grew up around all his doings, and he was in effect regarded as a god. He was also said to have been the 25th in a line of buddhas, each sent to enlighten humanity when the truth became forgotten. A succession of buddhas implied the existence of a Buddha of the Future, or Maitreya, who is portrayed in this grey schist statue. Its missing right hand was doubtless making a sign of benediction, while the left holds a water-flask, symbolizing the future. Like the Buddha on page 12, this one is carved in the Gandhara style, which developed in north-western India as a result of contacts with the late Greek ('Hellenistic') style which permeated the Middle East; hence the un-Indian physiognomy of these sculptures, which are usually described as Greco-Buddhist. The drapery, though Hellenistic in treatment, is Indian in arrangement, leaving the chest bare.

◁ **Yakshi** 1st century AD

Sandstone

THIS IS SOMEWHAT LATER in date than the *yakshi* from Ahichchatra (page 11), but the carving style has become bolder and the forms – notably the large breasts and the hips – are much rounder and more sensuous. In this example the *yakshi* is shown grasping a branch and standing in the *tribangha* or triple-bend pose, which became one of the most familiar motifs in Indian art; so did the pearl hip-belt, the necklace and the absence of any substantial clothing. Despite its monumental air, the figure is quite small, appearing on a door-handle found at Mathura, which became the greatest art centre in northern India during the early centuries AD. The material used was the local pink sandstone, whose distinctive feature – a generous sprinkling of pale spots – is clearly visible here. The *yakshi* set the pattern for other female types in carving, notably the *shalabhanjika*, the devastatingly beautiful woman who can make a tree blossom merely by touching it with her foot.

◁ **Head of Shiva**
1st century AD

Sandstone

THIS HEAD COMES FROM Mathura, one of India's three main artistic centres during this period. At Gandhara, in what is now Afghanistan, a 'Greco-Buddhist' style developed which influenced artists at Mathura, far away (about 130 km/80 miles below Delhi) in northern India. The reason was that both centres were part of the Kushan empire which stretched across the north-west and the north; Peshawar, in the north-west, was the Kushan capital, but their winter residence was at Mathura. In many respects Mathura sculpture remained independent of Gandharan influence, but contacts between the two may explain why Mathura produced its earliest images of the Buddha at about the time that such images also appeared in the north-west. Here, some Greco-Buddhist elements (for example, the curly hair) have even been transferred to a head of the Hindu deity Shiva, shown with a crescent-moon ornament and a vertical 'third eye' in the middle of his forehead.

Detail

▷ **An Episode from the Life of the Buddha** 1st century AD

Limestone

DURING THE EARLY CENTURIES AD, Amaravati was the third great centre of Indian sculpture. Unlike Gandhara and Mathura, it was well beyond the influence of the Kushans: Amaravati belonged to the Andhra kingdom much further south, situated not far from the south-east coast of India. The great Buddhist *stupas* in the region were particularly lavishly decorated, and although they have been destroyed, superb reliefs have been recovered from the remains. They show that the Amaravati style was less 'classical' but more lively than that of its northern counterparts. The figures are less thick-set, although the sensuality of the females is extremely potent. The scene is crowded, and so arranged that the eye travels restlessly across it, creating a strong sense of movement; outside the picture, every available space is filled with plant and other decorative patterns. Such impressions of teeming, superabundant life recur again and again in Indian sculpture and architecture.

◁ **Head of the Buddha**
5th century AD

Sandstone

UNDER THE GUPTA DYNASTY (320-c 550), Indian sculpture achieved its 'classic moment', encapsulated in this work from Sarnath. Everything inessential has been eliminated from the face, so that the noble features of the Buddha are not overwhelmed by the stylized, decorative treatment of the hair. Though nowhere 'realistic', the head conveys an impression of inner life and spiritual concentration. The elongated ear-lobes are a convention, reminding the viewer that, before his great renunciation, the Buddha had once lived the life of a prince, his person weighed down by precious ornaments. His 'top knot' represents a cranial protruberance said to indicate the possession of exceptional spiritual insight. A great centre of Buddhist Gupta art, Sarnath had been a holy city ever since the Buddha himself, having achieved enlightenment, chose to give his first sermon there.

△ **Spectators** 5th century AD

Sandstone

BUDDHIST ART ACHIEVED a classic perfection during the Gupta period (opposite) but by its end the Buddhist religion was beginning to decline on the Indian subcontinent, although it had a great future before it in many other parts of the Far East. By contrast, Hinduism underwent a great revival, eventually absorbing Buddhism into its own complex religious and social system. Hindu sculpture also flourished under the Guptas, the most celebrated works being carved on the now-ruined walls of the Dashavatara Temple at Deogarh in central India. These portrayed the main Hindu deities, including a splendid recumbent Vishnu dreaming the universe into existence. This is a less portentous relief from Deogarh, showing lovers sitting at their ease, enjoying the delights of wine and the performances of musicians and dancers.

Detail

▷ **Mahavira** 6th-7th century

Painted panel

INDIA IS FAMOUS as the birthplace and battleground of great religions. Buddhism was in a sense a reaction against Hinduism, accepting its doctrine of reincarnation but rejecting the caste system and reliance upon a pantheon of gods. Remarkably, a near-contemporary of the Buddha, Mahavira (c540-468 BC), also preached a new doctrine and founded a new religion, known as Jainism. Mahavira shared the Buddha's indifference to the caste system, but laid more emphasis on an austere set of personal standards. A striking feature of his teaching is the absolute sacredness of life (*ahimsa*), which prompts Jains to do everything possible to avoid harming any creature, however microscopic. The portrait of Mahavira comes from a sanctuary in Khotan, just north of present-day Kashmir. Although a recorded historical figure, he has already been transformed into a godlike being with four arms, dwarfing the two bullocks beneath his throne. Like so many early Indian paintings, this one is in poor condition.

◁ **Avalokiteshvara**
9th-10th century

Basalt

THIS GODLIKE BEING, looming over his devotees in very much the same way as a Hindu deity like Sarasvati (page 26), illustrates the evolution of Buddhism away from its original simplicity. Avalokiteshvara, 'the Lord who looks down', is one of the *bodhisattvas*, enlightened beings who were first shown in art as the Buddha's companions. The *bodhisattva* had accumulated so much merit that he was capable of attaining Nirvana, but delayed his entry into bliss in order to help humankind. However, Avalokiteshvara, like the Maitreya (page 14) and even the Buddha himself, acquired the trappings and aura of a god – which, ironically, weakened Indian Buddhism, since it became less distinct from Hinduism and ill-equipped to survive the onslaught of Islam. This basalt figure from eastern India shows Avalokiteshvara with his conventional attributes, notably a seated figure of the supreme Buddha (*Amithaba*) in his crown and a large, stylized lotus in his left hand.

◁ Harihara Dancing
10th century

Stone

DESPITE ITS DAMAGED CONDITION, this is a fascinating work, strongly reminiscent of a dancer performing in a modern ballet; in particular, it resembles the kind of pose taken up by the famous Nijinsky. Music and dancing were central features of Hindu ritual, in the great temples and also at the level of village festivals. Indian music achieved a complexity and sophistication that has only recently been recognized in the West, while dancing has always had a dramatic and symbolic function, so that every pose and gesture is meaningful. Ultimately, the entire cosmos could be understood in terms of the dance (page 28). Harihara is a composite deity, half Vishnu (Hari) and half Shiva (Hara). This sculpture comes from the territory of the Pratihara dynasty in central India; other splendid carvings of the god and his doings survive on the walls of the ruined temple to Harihara at Osian in Rajasthan.

Detail

▷ **The Goddess Sarasvati** 12th century

Marble

SARASVATI IS THE CONSORT OF BRAHMA, 'the father of gods and men' and the principal deity in the Hindu trinity. Although she seems to have originated as a river goddess, her great role is as Sarasvati Vagdevi, 'goddess of speech'. Since recitation and declamation were central to the religious and scholarly tradition, this associated her with intellectual pursuits, and she is credited with the invention of the Sanskrit alphabet and the patronage of poetry, music and learning. The blurred lines between Indian religions are illustrated by the fact that this statue was actually made in Rajasthan by Jain craftsmen. As usual, the goddess is portrayed as a beautiful young woman with four arms, carrying various symbolic objects. Surrounded by small attendants and devotees, she holds up the prime symbol of literature and art, a book whose manuscript pages were made from long palm leaves, sewn together and 'bound' in wooden boards.

Detail

▷ **Shiva Dancing** 12th century

Bronze

A DISTINCTIVE ARTISTIC TRADITION developed in the south of India, where the inhabitants were Dravidians, mainly descended from the pre-Aryan population. At a time in the Middle Ages when Indian art was tending to become stale, the Dravidians produced bronze sculptures that were outstanding in their balance and harmony. These qualities are maintained in this famous image of the god Shiva as the Lord of the Dance, despite the difficulties involved in his possession of four arms. The hoop of flames represents the cosmos, for when Shiva dances, one world dies and another is born. This is symbolized by the drum and the flame which he holds in his upper hands. He dances on a demon dwarf, representing ignorance, and among his outspread hair floats the figure of Ganga, goddess of the Ganges, who looks on the Lord of the Dance with her hands placed together in an attitude of worship.

▷ **The Goddess Kali**
12th century

Bronze

LIKE HER DANCING HUSBAND Shiva (page 28), this figure of Kali comes from the south of India; it provides an even better example of the classical simplicity of the Dravidian bronzes produced during the Chola period (9th to 12th centuries). Hindu gods and goddesses exist under many names, each representing one or more facets or incarnations of the divine. This fact reflects the Indian conviction that contraries – good and evil, birth and death, creation and destruction – are only aspects of a single undifferentiated process. Shiva's wife is Parvati, beautiful yet ascetic; but she is also Durga, ferocious in battle, and Kali, 'the Black One', a destroyer with an insatiable lust for blood. Although she is most often shown as a horrific figure, festooned with severed heads and limbs, in the south she was usually shown as a beauty, her bad habits only hinted at by her fangs; but in this calm and lovely work even they are absent.

▷ **Radha and Krishna** c1550

Paint on paper

UNTIL VERY RECENT TIMES, all Indian paintings took the form of frescoes, or of miniatures done for books and albums. The earliest surviving miniatures were painted on long, narrow palm leaves, strung together and enclosed within wooden covers. Paper was not introduced until the 13th century, and only became the norm in the 15th. The painting shown here is one of a group done at Mewar, a Hindu kingdom in Rajputana (western India). It illustrates a poem, the *Gita Govinda*, which describes Krishna's amours with milkmaids, of whom the chief was Radha. Krishna, one of the best-loved Hindu gods, is always shown as blue-skinned. Despite its naïve-seeming style, this is a pleasing picture which is rather effectively laid out. The details are striking (for example the peacock and the border of fish, waves and flowers), yet most of the expected background has been eliminated in favour of flat colours, notably the bright red that focuses attention on the god and his love.

▷ **Krishna Dancing on a
Snake** 16th-17th century

Bronze

THE DEVELOPMENT OF HINDU
ART was severely disrupted by the
Muslim invasions of the 13th
century. Hindu traditions survived
best in Rajputana, which
produced some notable painting,
and in the far south, where
bronzes of a high quality
continued to be made. However,
the Dravidian style became
increasingly decorative, and the
group shown here, though fanciful
and vigorous, is less poised and
harmonious than earlier works.
The subject comes from the
boyhood of Krishna, which was
spent among herders; although an
incarnation of Vishnu, in his
human form he needed protection
from his murderous uncle, and so
remained incognito until he
reached maturity. Even as a boy
he performed amazing feats,
destroying demons, pulling up
trees and, here, vanquishing the
many-headed snake Kalilya. He
owed his great popularity among
Hindus to his reputation as a
prankster, stealing the clothes of
bathing girls and luring maidens
to him by playing the flute;
despite his fickleness and
amorality, his erotic adventures
were much admired.

▷ Rustam Slaying Asdiv of Mazandaran Late 16th century

Paint on paper

THE EARLIEST MUSLIM INCURSIONS into India began in the early 8th century, when Arab armies captured the north-western region of Sind. But most of the sub-continent was unaffected until invasions starting in the late 12th century led to the establishment of a Muslim dynasty in Delhi and the importation of elements of Persian culture. These became far stronger after Babur established the Mughal empire in 1525-26. The jewel-like delicacy of Persian miniature painting was copied and modified by Indian artists, who created a new 'Indo-Persian' style. The scene shown here was painted in the Deccan, but the text is that of a Persian classic, the *Shah-Nama* by Firdusi, and the style is almost entirely Persian. The hero of this episode, Rustam, was the Persian Hercules, whose legendary exploits included this St-George-like feat, the slaying of the white monster Asdiv.

Detail

▷ **The Infant Akbar is Presented to Humayun** c1590

Paint on paper

A NEW ERA BEGAN IN 1525-26, when the Mughal leader Babur descended on India from his capital at Kabul. By the time of his death in 1530 he had conquered much of the north-west, and the Mughal empire endured and prospered despite the vicissitudes experienced by Babur's son Humayun (1530-56). At the lowest point in his career Humayun became an exile at the Persian court; and when his fortunes improved, he returned to Kabul, and eventually India, bringing with him Persian artists. Consequently, the cultural outlook of the Mughal court became Persian rather than central Asian, modified in time by native Indian influences. Humayun was obsessed by astrology, and it is said that when his son Akbar was born the child's horoscope was so propitious that the Emperor danced for joy. On this occasion the horoscope was not wrong; the scene in which Akbar is presented to his father at Kabul comes from the *Akbar-Nama*, a biography of Akbar which records all his triumphs.

◁ **Portrait of a Man** 1589

Paint on paper

THE MUGHAL EMPERORS maintained studios in which scores of artists were employed. Thanks to the relative tolerance of the early Mughals, many of these artists were Hindus who, having absorbed Persian techniques, made their own contribution to the development of Indo-Islamic art. The court painter was, among other things, a visual historian, producing set-piece records of events and individual portraits with recognizable features (by contrast with the generalized images made of, for example, the Buddha). The painter's role was important enough for his name to be attached to one of his works, although not so important that it was done on a regular basis. This portrait is by Abul Hasan, the leading Mughal artist under Akbar and his son Jahangir. According to Jahangir, a great connoisseur, the two great artists of his own time were Abul Hasan and Mansur (one of whose works is shown on page 49).

◁ **The Death of Adham Khan**
c1590

Paint on paper

ALTHOUGH THE ASTROLOGERS
had predicted greatness and good
fortune for him, the 13-year-old
Akbar had to fight hard even to
hold the throne he inherited from
his father in 1556. Akbar's greatest
assets were devotedly loyal
advisers and his own
extraordinary energy. Faced with
two rival aspirants to his throne,
he marched to war, only to hear
that a third, Himu, had seized
Delhi. Akbar returned and on the
5th November 1556 defeated
Himu at the battle of Panipat. In
the following year Akbar deposed
his two rivals and for a time
allowed himself to be ruled by his
advisers. After he took over the
reins of government in 1560, he
was faced with a final challenge
from within by his foster-brother,
Adham Khan, who murdered
Akbar's chief minister – shown
bottom left, lying in his blood –
and attempted to assassinate the
Emperor himself. Akbar fended
him off and ordered that he
should be flung headlong from
the terrace. This dramatic
moment is recorded in a miniature
from the *Akbar-Nama*.

Detail

▷ **Akbar Crossing the River Ganges** c1590

Paint on paper

AKBAR (1556-1605) WAS the most remarkable of all the Mughals. During his 49-year reign he expanded his shaky north-western dominions into an empire that stretched from Persia to the Bay of Bengal. By the 1570s the Rajput kings in the west had been subdued or had prudently recognized Mughal supremacy. Within the next ten years Bengal, beyond the Ganges, had been conquered. And during the rest of Akbar's reign, Mughal expansion continued to the north and west, and south into the Deccan. Meanwhile, the Emperor's artists were kept busy recording the legends of the past and the feats of the present. Painting seemed to take on something of Akbar's own immense vitality, sacrificing the exquisite quality of the Persian tradition for a new energy and sense of action. These are very apparent in the scene from the *Akbar-Nama* in which the Emperor, his followers, and their elephants and horses force their way across the Ganges.

Detail

▷ **Building the Red Fort** c1590

Paint on paper

AKBAR WAS A GREAT BUILDER, tackling current projects with characteristic vigour and instigating new ones, in new places, with something of the restlessness of his nomad forebears. Among his most impressive monuments are the city of Fatehpur Sikri and the Red Fort at Agra. 'Fort' hardly describes this huge palace-complex-cum-castle, standing 21 metres (69 feet) high and protected by walls two km (1.2 miles) long and a ditch 10 metres (33 feet) deep. Painting is our prime source of information about everyday life in Mughal times, and this illustration from the *Akbar-Nama* shows a range of building activities, so zealously pursued that we can be certain that the workmen were well aware of the artist's presence. Everybody is busily employed weighing, knocking, nailing, carrying materials up ramps, and laying the stones and mortar; meanwhile, fresh building supplies are arriving by water and in a cart being drawn by a rather undernourished-looking bullock.

Detail

▷ **A Siege in Progress** c1590

Paint on paper

THIS THRILLING, VERTIGINOUS battle-piece from the *Akbar-Nama* conveys the heat and haste of action in masterly fashion: the rugged terrain, the press of men urging on the bullocks as they haul the big siege-gun into position, the babble of voices, beating of drums and roar of the artillery. Two of the gunners crouch behind a screen, presumably to protect themselves from the effects of the most powerful cannon. In the midst of all this furious activity, the artist has rather cheekily placed a few birds and beasts who seem to be interested spectators, rather implausibly unabashed by the turmoil; one, quite close to the guns, is a mountain goat. Akbar's men are besieging the Rajput town of Ranthambhor, whose commander surrendered to the Emperor on generous terms, so that this was in reality one of the Mughals's less bloodthirsty operations.

Detail

▷ **Surjam Hada Submitting to Akbar** c1590

Paint on paper

HERE IS THE GREAT AKBAR in all his glory – in the field, enjoying another triumph, but also at his ease in a tent like a canopied open-air palace. The state which the emperors kept in wartime is also hinted at in the corner of *A Siege in Progress* (page 42). Like their nomad ancestors, the Mughals travelled to war with an entourage, but one which their imperial status had caused to swell to the size of a second army. The scene shows the Mughal artist's delight in picturing throngs of people and gorgeously decorated fabrics and carpeting; and for good measure there is a townscape with a procession of horsemen leaving from the main gate. Akbar, the patron of poets and painters, never learned to read and write, but used others as his instruments. Painters followed his instructions, and his biography, the *Akbar-Nama*, if not actually dictated to its author, the minister Abul Fazl, certainly provides a faithful reflection of the Emperor's self-image.

▷ **Prince Salim Surprised by a Lion** c1595-1600

Paint on paper

PRINCE SALIM, AKBAR'S ELDEST SON, is out hunting when a lion, with unusual temerity, suddenly attacks him, despite the fact that he is seated high on the back of an elephant. The Prince reacts courageously (at any rate in this picture by a court artist), defending himself with the butt of his rifle. Apart from the very precise rectangular rip made by the lion in the elephant's fabric covering, the scene is extremely convincing, showing once again that Akbar's artists were masters at combining colourful decoration and pattern-making with vigorous human drama. Salim became increasingly impatient to replace his ageing father, only drawing back on the brink of outright rebellion when challenged by Akbar's minister (and biographer), Abul Fazl – whom Salim then arranged to have assassinated. Fortunately for him, he was Akbar's only possible successor, since his brother was a chronic alcoholic who died in 1604. The following year, Salim succeeded his father as emperor, taking the name Jahangir, 'World-Seizer'.

◁ **Asaveri with a Cobra**
1605

Paint on paper

THIS MINIATURE FROM Udaypur
in Rajasthan shows the
persistence of the Hindu painting
tradition, and is in the starkest
possible contrast to
contemporary works by Mughal
artists. Its purpose – the
illustration of a musical mode –
highlights the close links between
Hindu art, music and poetry.
Indian musical scales consist of
ragas and *raginis*, which are
conceived of as male and female.
They are also associated with
colour values and with states of
mind or situations. Medieval
Indian poets composed series of
poems, called *ragamalas*,
describing these situations, and
painters in turn illustrated the
poems. The heroine of this
painted *ragamala* is Asaveri,
whom the poet pictures 'with
shining dark skin, adorned with
peacock feathers and a necklace
of rare, splendid pearls'. Seated
on a mountain top, she has
dragged a snake from its hole and
is about to use it as a girdle.
Although so highly stylized that it
is almost cartoon-like, this is a
very lively picture.

◁ **A European and His Servants** c1605

Paint on paper

MOST HUMAN CULTURES have found outsiders faintly ridiculous, or menacing, or both. The Mughal artist's view of Europeans is, all things considered, quite a kindly one, although the bent knees and rounded backs of the servants – servility in the European style – evidently struck him as worth emphasizing. The naïve air of the painting contrasts strongly with the confidence of contemporary Mughal art, possibly indicating that the subject matter was still too unfamiliar to be treated with real assurance; many of the details suggest that the artist was basing his work on a European original – perhaps an engraving – rather than direct observation. The Portuguese navigator Vasco da Gama and his crew were the first Europeans to reach India by sea, landing at Calicut in 1498; but the earliest European contacts with the Mughals in the north occurred later, in the 1570s.

▷ **A Jesuit** 1610

Paint on paper

AMONG THE EARLIEST EUROPEANS to reach the Mughal empire were Jesuit missionaries, sent from the Portuguese enclave at Goa at the request of the Emperor Akbar. They arrived at Fatehpur Sikri 'to convert the inhabitants', but found that the Emperor, though deeply interested in religion, was not necessarily inclined to accept any single creed as the final truth. His attitude disconcerted the missionaries, who seem to have been more angered by Akbar's open-mindedness than they might have been by obstinate opposition; nevertheless there were new missions during the 1590s. This portrait is far more natural than the painting of Europeans (opposite), perhaps only because the artist was more talented. In this instance he was Mansur, whom the Emperor Jahangir went so far as to call 'the Wonder of the Age'; and he has certainly shown the Jesuit, not as an oddity, but as he might have seen himself. Everything from the skin tones to the rosary is well observed, so no doubt the foreigner really did at least yield to Indian custom in the matter of his footwear.

Detail

◁ **The Weighing of Prince Khurram** c1615

Paint on paper

THIS PAINTING GIVES US a direct entrée into the Mughal court at the height of its splendour. It is alive with opulent details, including the cabinet at the back, filled with objects that look like porcelains and other imports from China. At the same time, the canopy and garden, real or imaginary, give the scene an open-air feeling which the Mughals seem always to have valued, presumably as a memory of their nomad origins. The miniature illustrates an episode, recorded in the memoirs of the Emperor Jahangir, which can be dated to 1607. Warned by his astrologers that a crucial period was at hand, and recalling that his son Khurram had been in poor health, Jahangir ordered that on his 16th birthday the boy should be weighed against quantities of gold and other precious metals, which were then distributed among holy men and the poor. Khurram survived to become the Emperor Shah Jahan (page 52).

1-CENTURY
...one during the
...ign of Shah Jahan (1628-58).
Although it may well be a good
likeness, the impression of the
Emperor it conveys could hardly
be more idealized. He is pictured
with a flower in one hand, sitting
in a kind of miniature pavilion
which is open to the air. The floral
patterns are exquisite and, as so
often, the calligraphy is beautiful
in its own right and fully
integrated into the overall design.
In reality, Shah Jahan was as
capable of excess as any of his
ancestors or descendants,
rebelling against his father and
murdering a number of relatives –
including his own brother – in
order to secure the throne. During
his reign Mughal power showed
signs of waning, and a Muslim
reaction began against the wise
religious tolerance of Akbar and
Jahangir. By contrast, Mughal
painting remained as skilful as
ever, although it has been argued
that its very perfection
represented a dead end.

▷ **Shah Jahan and Mumtaz Mahal**

Paint on paper

THIS UNDATED MINIATURE SHOWS the Mughal emperor Shah Jahan and his favourite wife, Mumtaz Mahal. The Mughals were far from being faithful husbands, and they also exercised their legal right to be polygamists, if only because marriage was, among other things, a useful diplomatic device for cementing alliances. But they were nevertheless capable of strong attachments, and Jahangir's queen, Nur Jahan, had such a hold over him that she was able to exercise effective political power during his later years. Mumtaz Mahal had a less spectacular career, but on her death in 1632, giving birth to her 14th child, Shah Jahan built her the most famous of all mausolea, the Taj Mahal (page 55). Legend pictures the emperor, imprisoned by his own son during the last eight years of his life, as gazing mournfully from the Red Fort at Agra on the tomb of his beloved wife.

◁ **The Taj Mahal** 1632-54

THE WORLD-FAMOUS TAJ MAHAL
is actually a mausoleum, built at
Agra by the Mughal emperor
Shah Jahan for his favourite wife,
Mumtaz Mahal ('Jewel of the
Palace'), who died in 1632. The
main structure was probably
complete within four or five
years, but the entire scheme took
over 20 years. In essentials, the
Taj Mahal is an octagonal
building crowned with an onion
dome and extending on its
platform to four corner minarets.
Its plan was not new, but was
based on the tomb of Shah
Jahan's great-grandfather,
Humayun. The dramatic
difference lay in the lavish use of
a dazzling white marble facing,
which lightened and lifted the
building, giving it a dream-like
quality in spite of its immense
size. The Jumna River flows on
one side of the Taj Mahal; the
main facade lies behind the
lovely formal garden, broken by
water-courses, which is perhaps a
vital element in the sense of
enchantment which generations
of visitors have experienced
at this spot.

Detail

▷ **A Polo Match** Mid-17th century

Paint on paper

OUR KNOWLEDGE OF EVERYDAY LIFE in India is deficient in many respects, in part because so much Hindu and Buddhist art was created for exclusively religious purposes. Fortunately Mughal attitudes were quite different: the emperors delighted in the pageantry and pleasures of their lives, and in seeing them recorded for posterity. Though limited by the fact that it is a court art, the Mughal miniature gives us a lively picture of the age. The artist who painted this scene was interested in all its incidents – not just the aristocrats at play on splendid mounts, but also the servants bringing fresh sticks and the player being cooled off with a fan. Polo originated in Central Asia as a mimic battle; Muslim invaders introduced it to India, and by Mughal times it had become a civilized, aristocratic pastime. Later, in the 1860s, British planters and officers in India took it up, and by the 1880s it had become an international competitive sport.

◁ **Muhammad Azam** c1680

Paint on paper

MUHAMMAD AZAM (1653-1707) was the third son of the puritanical Mughal emperor Aurangzeb. The Emperor shut down the royal workshops which had produced so many superb miniature paintings, and the scores of artists who had been employed in them had to seek work at other Indian courts. Consequently their dispersal did not bring the Mughal artistic tradition to an abrupt end, although it was inevitably weakened in the long run. This portrait of Muhammad Azam holding a falcon is as fine as any Mughal miniature, but it was painted in the Deccan, an area of central India that Aurangzeb occupied but never managed to pacify; in fact the emperor's obsessive and ruinously expensive efforts to suppress one Deccani revolt after another were the main reason for the rapid decline of Mughal power after his death in 1707. One of the victims in the battles for the succession was Muhammad Azam, who perished at the hands of his brother, Bahadur Shah.

▷ **Aurangzeb at Prayer**

Paint on paper

LIKE HIS FATHER AND
GRANDFATHER, Aurangzeb waded
through the blood of his brothers
and relations in order to become
Mughal emperor; unlike them, he
took power before the death of his
father, Shah Jahan, who spent his
final years (1658-66) in prison. But
as emperor, Aurangzeb soon
became a pillar of Muslim
orthodoxy, encouraging the trend
towards the persecution of
Hindus; despite the military
successes he achieved during his
lifetime, his reign alienated the
majority of the Indian population
and fatally weakened the fabric of
Mughal society. His influence on
painting was equally negative,
since he patronized the arts for
only a few years before becoming
convinced that the representation
of human beings was against
Islamic law. So there is a
paradoxical appropriateness in
this 'sinful' yet pious image of the
emperor, his sword beside him and
a fly-whisk in his hand, kneeling
on his prayer mat.

△ **Krishna Holding up Mount Govardhan** c1690

Paint on paper

THIS ILLUSTRATES A very well-known Hindu myth which, like many myths, preserves the memory of a real historical event. In this instance the event was the dethronement of Indra, along with other ancient Vedic gods worshipped by the Aryans, in favour of Vishnu-Krishna and the other deities of an evolving Hinduism. The myth relates that the sky god Indra became angry with his former worshippers when they began to sacrifice to Krishna.

Indra unleashed a terrible storm on them, but Krishna effortlessly raised the mountain, using it as an umbrella to shield his followers; and Indra was compelled to admit his rival's superiority. The miniature was painted in the western desert state of Bikaner, whose artists were influenced by the Mughal school but nevertheless produced distinctive work of their own. The details – especially the cow giving birth – are both curious and charming.

▷ **Swimming to a Lover**
18th century

Paint on paper

WITH THE DECLINE OF THE Muslim Mughal empire, provincial rulers, mostly Hindu, were able to assert their political and artistic independence. A variety of schools of painting sprang up in the Rajput kingdoms of the west, and also in the numerous Punjab Hills states much further north. This painting from Rajasthan has a curious, rather quirky air. The man, having laid aside his shoes and weapons, plays the pipes abstractedly, apparently unaware of any possible consequences. The woman breasts the stream as if in a trance, perhaps drawn by the music rather than by the sight of her lover: Hindus who looked at the picture would certainly be reminded of the exploits of the god Krishna, whose fluting made him irresistible to women. It may be significant that the seated ascetic in the foreground is painted blue, like Krishna himself in Indian paintings. The picture is full of delightful natural details, well worth close scrutiny.

Detail

▷ **The Submission of Kaliya** First half of the 18th century

Paint on paper

LATE IN THE 17TH CENTURY, schools of miniature painting developed for the first time at a number of centres in the Punjab Hills. The style was known as Pahari, and the ever-popular adventures of Krishna provided much of the subject matter, as in this painting from the state of Basohli. It shows Krishna in his moment of triumph over Kaliya, the king of the snake deities, after a struggle which the god won by dancing on the hooded head of his opponent. The wives of Kaliya are also worshipping Krishna. This was one of the god's bloodless victories, for, once vanquished, the snakes became his loyal devotees. The incident is still celebrated every year at the Nagapanchami festival, when paintings like this one (though in cheaper, more disposable versions) are put on public display to protect their owners from the unwelcome attentions of snakes.

Detail

▷ **A Lady Waiting for her Lover** c1760

Paint on paper

This is an unusually potent mood painting from the Punjab Hills school in the north-west. The subject illustrates the abiding Indian interest in the arts and incidents of love, manifested in the early centuries AD by the celebrated *Kama Sutra*, which was itself said to be a mere abridgement of a much earlier work. Here, the lady's feelings about her absent lover are conveyed not only by her expression and attitude, but most poignantly by the brilliant touches of red on her lips and nails, emphasizing the care with which she has prepared herself for his coming. Evidently he is long overdue, for although the lady is wide awake, her maid has fallen asleep and seems to be having agreeable dreams. The thunder and lightning are rendered in a sketchy, dramatic style that makes an effective contrast with the still, sorrowful atmosphere of the scene below.

Detail

▷ **Durga in Combat** 1750

Paint on paper

THIS SCENE IS AN INTERESTING example of what could happen when Mughal influences were brought to bear on traditional Hindu culture, represented by a miniature painting from the Rajput state of Bikaner. The subject is the battle between the goddess Durga and the demon Mahishasura. Durga's name signifies 'she who is difficult to contend with', and she is the battle-seeking incarnation of Parvati, wife of the great god Shiva. Durga's ten arms have been reduced to a more manageable four, and she is painted in a refined style derived from Mughal art. Her most striking gesture is hieratic rather than warlike, although in her other three hands she carries a dagger, a sword and a lance in the form of a snake. Mahishasura, however, is a fanged, eight-armed demon in the traditional mould, snarling defiance despite the fact that his steed is succumbing to Durga's lion mount. The indispensable gore is provided by the decapitated warrior on the ground.

Detail

▷ **A Prince Out Riding** c1751

Paint on paper

THIS MINIATURE WAS PAINTED in the northern Punjab state of Jammu, and probably portrays the Raja Balwant Singh. The artist was Nainsukh (active 1740-51), who certainly produced a number of portraits of Balwant Singh; his figures tended to be small, as here, and sometimes minuscule. In one curious picture, the rajah is a tiny figure standing on the formidably high walls of his palace, which occupy almost the entire available space. Like the Mughals, Bulwant Singh evidently believed in taking his pleasures with him wherever he went, for apart from his falcon and huntsman he is accompanied by musicians, a servant to carry the hukka which he smokes even on the move, and some feminine company. The riders make their way through a delightful carpet of flowers, in a landscape with strangely schematized vegetation. The rather faint figures of retainers and dogs stand in the distance, and the vivid red of sun-inflamed clouds can just be glimpsed over the line of the hills.

Detail

▷ **Celebrating the Festival of Holi** c1780

Paint on paper

ONE OF THE LEADING ARTISTIC CENTRES among the Punjab Hill states was Guler. Its position, not far from the plains and the imperial court, ensured that Mughal influences were quickly absorbed, and that unemployed Mughal artists were warmly received. Consequently Guler miniatures became well-known for their refinement, while maintaining a characteristic Hindu boldness and vigour. Chaos appears to prevail in the painting shown here; but it is a cleverly composed chaos. Holi, the spring festival, is being celebrated to the music of drums, horns, strings and tambourine. In traditional fashion, the merrymakers are flinging red powder from a large tub over one another, and using bamboo syringes to squirt water all over the place. In this instance, the participants are the blue-skinned god Krishna, his favourite Radha, and assorted enticing ladies. Although slightly damaged, this is one of the most lively representations we have of everyday life among Hindus two centuries ago.

Detail

▷ **The Search for Sita** 1780

Paint on paper

THE SCENES IN THIS miniature painting from Kangra illustrate episodes from the *Ramayana*, one of two ancient Indian epics (the other is the *Mahabarhata*) dating back over 2000 years. The main story-line in the *Ramayana* concerns the wanderings of Rama, his wife Sita, and Rama's brother, Lakshmana. Denied his rightful position as king of Ayodhya, Rama leads his companions to a forest refuge. When he rejects the advances of a female demon, her vengeful brother, Ravana, king of Lanka, carries off Sita, who is only found after many adventures and much help from the monkey king Hanuman and other animal allies. The painting is an example of continuous representation – that is, a narrative with several episodes shown in a single picture. Though now unfamiliar, it was common in western painting until quite late in the Renaissance. Where the episodes are thematic – like the search going on in this picture – the device can be very effective.

▷ **Krishna Adorning Radha's Breast** c1780

Paint on paper

THE LEADING PUNJAB HILLS SCHOOL between about 1775 and 1825 was at Kangra, where the rajah, Sansar Chand, was a passionate lover of painting. Under his generous patronage, the Kangra painters developed an intensely poetic style that imbued the traditional subjects, mainly taken from the life of Krishna, with a new romantic appeal, especially when they were set in lovely landscapes. The story of Krishna and the milkmaid Radha was a perennial favourite, bringing with it an illicit thrill, since Radha was a married woman who abandoned her husband for Krishna, despite his notorious fickleness. Like most such stories, the amours of Krishna can be interpreted in symbolic terms, culminating in union with the divine, when the god's generosity with his favours appears in another light; but it can be questioned whether symbolism was uppermost in the minds of Indian painters. Here, the intimacy of the lovers stands out against the wide landscape with its distant view of a city.

◁ **Shooting Tigers** c1790

Paint on paper

THE STATE OF KOTAH, in the Punjab Hills, produced a distinctive school of artists, notable for their renderings of animals, hunting scenes and landscapes. As in this miniature, the style was hard and clear-cut almost to the point of caricature, showing an obsessive interest in detail and creating strange, rhythmic forms such as the rock formations along the upper edge of the picture. The result has been convincingly likened to the paintings of the French 'primitive' painter, the Douanier Rousseau (1844-1910). Here, on a moonlit night, Rajah Umed Singh and his chief minister, Zalim Singh, are ensconced in a tree-hide above a clearing; a tiger is attacking the buffalo tethered there to attract it, and the two men are firing with their long muskets. The depiction of such a scene, featuring real people, indicates the presence of strong Mughal or western influence.

△ **A Sikh Prince Hunting** 1830-40

Paint on paper

BY ABOUT 1820 IT WAS becoming clear that the British would be the new paramount power in India. Coincidentally or otherwise, the tradition of miniature painting was losing most of its vitality, although a few centres such as Kangra would turn out good-quality work for a little longer. Meanwhile the warlike Sikhs moved into the Punjab, acquired a taste for painting, and for a time produced miniatures that expressed a definite vigour. This hunting scene is a kind of composite, featuring several activities simultaneously: a leopard-shoot from a raised platform, a boar hunt on horseback, and a chase whose climax will probably take place off the page. Despite European influences on the style of the painting, rank rather than realism determines the way in which it is organized: although their figures overlap, the hunters are all the same size (and therefore effectively in the same plane), whereas an exaggerated perspective shrinks the ranks of soldier-retainers into rows of tiny toys.

ACKNOWLEDGEMENTS

The publisher would like to thank the following for their kind permission to reproduce the paintings in this book:

Bridgeman Art Library, London/National Museum of India, New Delhi: 8, 9, 10, 11, 13, 14, 17, *18*, 19, 20, 21, 25, *26*, 27, *28*, 29, 30, 31, 33, 49, *66*, 67, *72*, 73, 78; /**British Museum, London**: 12, 24, *34*, 35; /**Museo de Muttra, India/Index, Barcelona**: 15; /**British Library, London**: *22*, 23, 48, 50, *51*, 60; /**Victoria and Albert Museum, London**: 32, 36, 37, *38*, 39, *40*, 41, *42*, 43, *44*, 45, 47, *56*, 57, 58, 61, *62*, 63, *64*, 65, *68*, 69, *70*, 71, 76-77; /**Christie's, London**: 46; /**Private Collection**: 52 *(also used on front cover, back cover detail and half-title page detail)*, 74-75; /**Bridgeman Art Library, London**: 54-55; /**Bibliotheque Nationale, Paris**: 59;

NB: Numbers shown in italics indicate a picture detail.

Every effort has been made to trace the copyright holders and we apologise in advance for any unintentional omissions. We would be pleased to insert the appropriate acknowledgement in any subsequent edition of this publication.